EXPERT SYSTEMS

DESIGN, APPLICATIONS AND TECHNOLOGY

COMPUTER SCIENCE, TECHNOLOGY AND APPLICATIONS

Additional books in this series can be found on Nova's website
under the Series tab.

Additional e-books in this series can be found on Nova's website
under the eBooks tab.

COMPUTER SCIENCE, TECHNOLOGY AND APPLICATIONS

EXPERT SYSTEMS

DESIGN, APPLICATIONS AND TECHNOLOGY

DARREL RYAN
EDITOR

science publishers
New York

Library of Congress Cataloging-in-Publication Data

ISBN: 978-1-53612-503-0

Published by Nova Science Publishers, Inc. † New York

CONTENTS

PREFACE

The use of unconventional methods of artificial intelligence is the modern trend in the computer support of the solution of the decision-making methods. These methods are based on the use of knowledge of skilled professionals – experts, where this knowledge forms the basis for their high-quality knowledge mental models. Chapter One introduces the expert systems used for the simulation of the decision-making activity of experts when dealing with complex tasks. In terms of theory, the expert knowledge method is used. The introduced expert systems are able to effectively use uncertainties which take their source from inaccurate, incomplete, inconsistent input data, vague concepts of linguistic formulations of the rules, and uncertain knowledge. Chapter Two proposes a solution for heterogeneous data source integration in the information standard formats, based on Rule Based Expert System (RBES) to implement a metadata mining process. Later, it describes the process of automatic modelling in which the proposed RBES support in the data mining technique applications, based on the results of metadata mining process. Finally, it describes the application issues of the proposed solution in real cases. Chapter Three presents ARISTON, which is an integrated mathematical framework with all relevant parameters that constitute a fully automated, structured expert psychometric system for occupational guidance, aiming to identify and retrieve the professions which are nearest to the personality of an individual, while at the same time quantify all nearest "neighbouring" professions.

Chapter 1 – The chapter introduces the expert systems used for the simulation of the decision-making activity of experts when dealing with complex tasks. In terms of theory, the expert knowledge method is used. Knowledge is represented in the form of IF-THEN rules. In terms of technology, the pseudo-Bayesian approaches, probability theory, theory of fuzzy set mathematics and fuzzy logic are used for the purposes of formalizing the uncertainty and inference mechanisms. The application theme is focused on decision-making in the field of economy. Supplier choice support in the supply chain using the hierarchical fuzzy-oriented expert system technology. The global decision-making task is split into partial tasks and the expert modules are integrated into a 5-level hierarchical structure for their formalization. The impact determination of selected activities of economic entities on the corporate social responsibility using the probabilistically-oriented expert system technology. The linguistic rule-based modelling and the inference method are based on the pseudo-Bayesian approach. The determination of the selected key performance indicators of Balanced Scorecard customer dimension using the fuzzy-stochastic oriented expert system technology. The methods of calculating indicators and standards of quality of the outputs of the systems involving the human factor do not take into account their natural uncertainty. Hence, to determine the certain performance indicator in the frame of BSC by means of fuzzification of the input statistic figures of respondents with their subsequent processing by means of fuzzy arithmetic and fuzzy-logic. The efficiency of all the proposed decision-making expert systems is proven by a simulation exercise.

Chapter 2 – The arrival of new technologies related to Smart Grids and the resulting ecosystem of applications and management systems pose challenges or problems to be solved. In this way, the compatibility with databases of the traditional and the new management systems, related to initiatives of new technologies, have given rise to different formats and architectures. Due to this, a heterogeneous data source integration system is essential to update these systems for the new Smart Grid reality. In this sense, there are several problems which need to be solved: information integration, incomplete data model definition, understanding of database models, evolution of technologies and modelling information. Additionally, it is necessary to take advantage of the information that Smart Grids provide. The Smart Grids must provide new services to the consumers and operators, integrating the information from all the partners, ensuring the information protection and security. At first, this chapter briefly treats an analysis of the proposed problems and makes a bibliographical review. Following this review, it proposes a solution for heterogeneous data source integration in the information standard formats, based on Rule Based Expert System (RBES) to implement a metadata mining process. Later, it describes the process of automatic modelling in which the proposed RBES support in the data mining technique applications, based on the results of metadata mining process. Finally, it describes the application issues of the proposed solution in real cases.

Chapter 3 – Within a national or indeed international socio-economic environment the ideal state of employment is defined as follows: a) Each person is employed in a sector of his preference and choice, b) the sector or still better the actual profession has a high degree of match with the personality of the employee, c) each employee is doing exactly what is needed and is also required by the society, and d) the society provides all the necessary education/training for all sectors. In other words, there is absolute balance between supply and demand of goods, services and labour. This chapter presents ARISTON, which is an integrated mathematical framework with all relevant parameters that constitute a fully automated, structured expert psychometric system for occupational guidance, aiming to identify and retrieve the professions which are nearest to the personality of an individual, while at the same time quantify all nearest "neighbouring" professions.

In: Expert Systems
Editor: Darrel Ryan

ISBN: 978-1-53612-503-0
© 2017 Nova Science Publishers, Inc.

Chapter 1

SOFT-COMPUTING TECHNOLOGIES IN ECONOMICS EXPERT SYSTEMS

M. Pokorny, M. Mensik, E. Chytilova, D. Bernardova and Z. Krisova

Department of Informatics and Applied Mathematics,
Moravian University College, Olomouc, Czech Republic

ABSTRACT

The chapter introduces the expert systems used for the simulation of the decision-making activity of experts when dealing with complex tasks. In terms of theory, the expert knowledge method is used. Knowledge is represented in the form of IF-THEN rules. In terms of technology, the pseudo-Bayesian approaches, probability theory, theory of fuzzy set mathematics and fuzzy logic are used for the purposes of formalizing the uncertainty and inference mechanisms. The application theme is focused on decision-making in the field of economy. Supplier choice support in the supply chain using the hierarchical fuzzy-oriented expert system technology. The global decision-making task is split into partial tasks and the expert modules are integrated into a 5-level hierarchical structure for their formalization. The impact determination of selected activities of economic entities on the corporate social responsibility using the probabilistically-oriented expert system technology. The linguistic rule-based modelling and the inference method are based on the pseudo-Bayesian approach. The determination of the selected key performance indicators of Balanced Scorecard customer dimension using the fuzzy-stochastic oriented expert system technology. The methods of calculating indicators and standards of quality of the outputs of the systems involving the human factor do not take into account their natural uncertainty. Hence, to determine the certain performance indicator in the frame of BSC by means of fuzzification of the input statistic figures of respondents with their subsequent processing by means of fuzzy arithmetic and fuzzy-logic. The efficiency of all the proposed decision-making expert systems is proven by a simulation exercise.

Keywords: artificial intelligence, decision-making, expert system, knowledge, uncertainty, fuzzy-logic, pseudo-probability, stochastic, supplier choice, corporate social responsibility, balanced scorecards

INTRODUCTION

The use of unconventional methods of artificial intelligence is the modern trend in the computer support of the solution of the decision-making methods [1]. These methods are based on the use of knowledge of skilled professionals – experts, where this knowledge forms the basis for their high-quality knowledge mental models. Language model expert systems are then created in order to formalize the mental models of experts in computing. The synthesis of expert systems is a special problem of knowledge engineering [2].

The chapter introduces the expert systems used for the simulation of the decision-making activity of experts when dealing with complex tasks. The introduced expert systems are able to effectively use uncertainties which take their source from inaccurate, incomplete, inconsistent input data, vague concepts of linguistic formulations of the rules, and uncertain knowledge.

From the design methods, the expert knowledge method is used. Knowledge is represented in the form of IF-THEN rules. In terms of technology, the pseudo-Bayesian approaches, probability theory, theory of fuzzy set mathematics and fuzzy logic are used for purposes of formalizing the uncertainty and inference mechanisms [3].

The application theme is focused on decision-making in the field of economy, namely supplier choice support in the supply chain (hierarchical fuzzy-oriented expert system technology), impact determination of selected activities of economic entities on the CSR (probabilistically-oriented expert system technology), and determination of the selected key performance indicator of BSC customer dimension (fuzzy-stochastic oriented expert system technology).

The first part of the chapter focuses on the issue of the choice of suppliers in the market environment. The global decision-making task is split into partial tasks; the expert modules are integrated into a 5-level hierarchical structure for their formalization. The chapter presents the structures of constituent language models and the implementation of the structure of expert systems in the MATLAB-Simulink program environment. The efficiency of the decision-making system is proven by the solution of a simulation exercise. Economic entities as integral parts of the social system have an impact on it. The complexity of structures and uncertainty of behaviour which are also conditioned by incorporating the human factor are the typical characteristics of economic entities and the social system.

The second part of the chapter deals with the synthesis of the abstract model of the expert for determining the level of corporate social responsibility of an enterprise (CSR). The linguistic rule-based modelling and inference method are based on the pseudo-Bayesian approach. The presented expert system is a relevant module of the built hierarchical structure aimed at the study of impacts of activities of economic entities on the social system.

Finally, the third part of the chapter is focused on dealing with the fact that the methods of calculating indicators and standards of quality of the outputs of the systems involving the human factor do not take into account the substantial property of the processed data – their natural uncertainty. Data which have their origin in the human evaluation of phenomena using the integer numerical values are a typical example of such a vagueness of overloaded information. Unconventional methods of soft-computing are able to complete numeric information with the degree of its uncertainty as well. In the chapter, these approaches are applied to determine a certain performance indicator in the frame of Balanced Scorecard by means of fuzzification of the input figures of respondents with their subsequent processing by means of fuzzy arithmetic and fuzzy-logic. Crisp figures are replaced by fuzzy numbers; their uncertainty is determined by using four fuzzy-logic expert subsystems. Rule-based knowledge bases are based on the expert hypotheses which can be expressed as the relation between the uncertainty of the respondent's answer and his mental characteristics and attitudes. Expert systems are implemented both in the FEL-Expert program and in the fuzzy arithmetic software system. The uncertainty of the resulting criteria creates new information which leads to improving the efficiency of their use in decision-making processes.

1. RULE-BASED KNOWLEDGE EXPERT MODELLING

Knowledge in the presented expert systems is represented by means of rules in the form of [3]

IF (premise) THEN (conclusion)

The IF-THEN rule is often written also in the form of

$$E \rightarrow H, \tag{1.1}$$

where E represents evidence and H means hypothesis, the arrow symbol is a symbol for the reasoning procedure.

The IF p THEN q rule does not mean the same as the implication $p \Rightarrow q$. In an expert system, the operation q is performed in case that p is fulfilled. On the other hand, the implication is defined by a truth table and, in natural language, its meaning can be expressed in several ways.

The part of the rule behind *IF* is called the antecedent or conditional part. This part can consist of a plurality of individual conditions (multiple antecedent). The part of the rule behind *THEN* is called the consequent and can also contain a consequent conjunction. In the conditional part, conjunctions AND and OR can occure, in the v consequential part, the conjunction AND can occure.

Rule-based systems differ from standard logical systems by non-monotonic reasoning and the possibility of processing uncertainty. Uncertainty can occure in the rule premises and it can apply to the rule as a whole. For example, in the rule

IF (PEOPLE's HEIGHT is LARGE) *THEN* (PEOPLE's WEIGHT is BIG),

in the antecedent, there is on one hand the uncertain concept LARGE, on the other hand, the rule itself does not always have to be valid.

Approaches to handling uncertainty in rule-based systems can be divided into two basic groups: approaches based on ad hoc models (pseudo-Bayesian approaches) and approaches based on theoretical principles, e.g., on the probability theory or fuzzy sets theory (fuzzy-logic approaches).

2. UNCERTAINTY REPRESENTATION AND PROCESSING TECHNOLOGY

Uncertainty is a typical feature of complex systems. The very nature of reality causes knowledge that we gain from it to be uncertain or vague. In terms of data uncertainty, it is missing or unavailable data, unreliable data (e.g., due to measurement errors), or inaccurate or inconsistent data representation; in terms of knowledge, the fact that knowledge does not have to be valid in all cases or knowledge can incude vague concepts.

In expert systems, uncertainty is usually expressed by numerical parametres which are called differently in various systems, e.g., weights, measures, degree of confidence, certainty factors. These numerical parametres are assigned to particular statements or rules. They are often within the interval $\langle 0,1 \rangle$ or $\langle -1,1 \rangle$.

Uncertainty is usually expressed by means of a single number or a pair of numbers. There are also systems which work with unceranities which are expressed qualitatively.

In this chapter, we use the technology of rule-based systems. When handling uncertainty, we encounter the following problems (problems of approximative inference): how to combine uncertain data in the premise of the rule, how to combine the uncertainty of the premise of the rule and the uncertainty of the rule as a whole, and how to set the uncertainty of the conclusion to which several rules lead.

2.1. Pseudo-Bayesian Modelling and Hypothesis Evaluation

In the chapter, we work with the *IF-THEN* rules expressing the relationship between the evidence E and hypothesis H (1.1). According to the Bayes´ theorem, for proving the validity of hypotheses the following applies [3, 4]

$$P(H \mid E) = \frac{P(E \mid H) . P(H)}{P(E)}$$

where $P(H \mid E)$ is the conditional probability of the validity of the hypothesis H, provided that the evidence E is fulfilled; $P(E \mid H)$ is the conditional probability of the validity of the evidence E, provided that the hypothesis H is fulfilled; $P(E)$ and $P(H)$ are a priori probabilities of the evidence E or rather hypothesis H.

Let us consider the relationship (1.1) in the form of the *IF-THEN* rule:

$$IF \langle prem \, ise \, E \rangle \; THEN \; \langle conclusion H \, \rangle \; . \qquad\qquad (2.1)$$

In the pseudo-Bayesian system, the uncertainty of the rule is expressed by means of two measures – the sufficiency measure L and necessity measure L' where:

$$L, \, L' \in \langle 0, \, 1 \rangle .$$

These measures can be seen as subjective weights which are set by an expert for each rule and which modify the rule (2.1) as:

$$IF \langle prem \, ise E \rangle \; THEN \; \langle conclusion H \, \rangle \, with \, (weight L) ELSE H \, with \, (weight \, L')$$

Instead of the stated measures, the expert can enter the probabilities $P(H \mid E)$, $P(H \mid not E)$, $P(not E \mid H)$ and $P(not E \mid not H)$, by means of which these measures are calculated thereafter:

$$L = \frac{P(E \mid H)}{P(E \mid not H)} \; , \qquad \hat{L} = \frac{P(not E \mid H)}{P(not E \mid not H)} \; .$$

Let us consider that the evidences E in the rules $E \Rightarrow H$ will not only acquire logical values "truth" (i.e., truth value 1) or "false" (truth value 0) but their validity will be evaluated as uncertain in a particular situation – by the truth values from the interval $\langle 0, 1 \rangle$. The degree of fulfilment of the evidence E will be expressed as:

$$P\,(E \mid E') \in \langle 0, 1 \rangle.$$

Then, we will get the relationship for determining $P(H \mid E')$ in the form of:

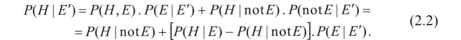

$$P(H \mid E') = P(H, E) \cdot P(E \mid E') + P(H \mid \text{not}\,E) \cdot P(\text{not}\,E \mid E') =$$
$$= P(H \mid \text{not}\,E) + \left[P(H \mid E) - P(H \mid \text{not}\,E)\right] \cdot P(E \mid E'). \quad (2.2)$$

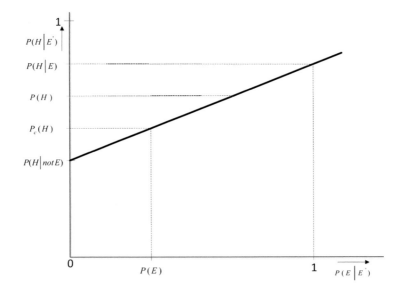

Figure 1. Linear function $P(H \mid E') = f(P(E \mid E'))/$

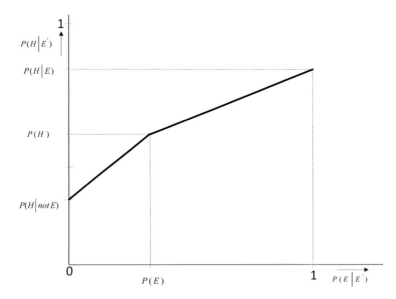

Figure 2. Broken-line approximation of function $P(H \mid E') = f(P(E \mid E'))$.

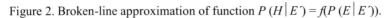

The values $P(H|E)$ and $P(H|\text{not}E)$ are entered by the expert directly or they can be calculated from L and $\hat{L}$. The equation represents a linear dependence between $P(H|E')$ and $P(E|E')$ and corresponds to the conventional Bayesian approach (Figure 1).

Since the expert enters $P(H|E)$ and $P(H|\text{not}E)$, $P(E)$ and $P(H)$ independently, from the mathematical point of view, the straight line according to the equation (2.2) is overdetermined and such a system of probability measures inconsistent. Therefore a solution that diverts from the conventional Bayesian approach is used – the system uses piecewise linear approximation (Figure 2).

For the calculation of $P(H|E')$ we use the following formula:

$$P(H|E') = P(H) + \frac{P(H|E) - P(H)}{1 - P(E)} \cdot (P(E|E') - P(E))$$

for $P(H|E) \geq P(H) \geq P(H|\text{not}E)$

$$P(H|E') = P(H|\text{not}E) + \frac{P(H) - P(H|\text{not}E)}{P(E)} \cdot P(E|E')$$

for $P(H|E) \leq P(H) \leq P(H|\text{not}E)$.

For the calculation of the probability evaluation of a logical combination of partial propositions, the pseudo-Bayesian model uses relations taken from the theory of fuzzy sets. For the conjunction, disjunction, and negation of premises, the following relationships are used [8]

$$P(E_1 \& E_2) = \min\{P(E_1), P(E_2)\}$$

$$P(E_1 \vee E_2) = \max\{P(E_1), P(E_2)\} \tag{2.3}$$

$$P(\text{not}\,E) = 1 - P(E)\,.$$

Advantages of Bayesian approaches: very good theoretical foundations, a well-defined semantics of decision-making. Disadvantages: the need for a large amount of probability data, risk of data incompleteness and inconsistency, presumption of the independence of the evidences Ei is rarely met in practice, possibility of the loss of information as a result of the description of uncertainty by one number, and difficulty of explaining.

The pseudo-Bayesian approach is used to evaluate target hypotheses in the FEL-Expert system [5], in which the implementation of the expert system is carried out – Subchapter 4.

2.2. Fuzzy-Logic Modelling and Reasoning

To formalize knowledge, fuzzy-oriented expert systems [6] use the widely known *IF-THEN* rules in the form of:

IF(antecedent) THEN (consequent).

Antecedents and consequents of rules are vague fuzzy propositions – their truth value is within the interval $\langle 0;1 \rangle$. The structure of fuzzy propositions contains language variables, their language values, and fuzzy logic conjunctions [7]. The following expression is a typical form:

$(X \text{ is } A)$

where X is a language variable and A is its corresponding language value. The uncertainty (vagueness) of language values is formalized by fuzzy sets.

In the rules of language models, fuzzy sets are used for the formalization of the meaning of the words of natural language (small, large, almost, nearly, etc.). Vagueness – i.e., uncertainty which has to be efficiently formalized by a fuzzy set – is a natural quality of the words.

In the fuzzy sets theory, in addition to the concept of absolute belonging or not belonging of an element to a set, the concept of partial belonging of an element to a set has been introduced. It is a generalization of the concept of the degree of belonging when we extend the definition filed of its values from two discrete (0, 1) (ordinary sets) to a closed interval <0, 1> (fuzzy sets)

$$\mu_F : U \rightarrow \langle 0,1 \rangle .$$

In practical application, the fuzzy set F of elements u is identified with its membership function $\mu_F(u)$. The membership function is mostly approximated by broken lines. A triangular approximation of a fuzzy set can be seen in Figure 3.

For language models, language variables which are quantified by language values are typical. The meaning of vague language values is formalized by membership functions of fuzzy sets.

The synthesis of the rule-based fuzzy model is carried out based on expert hypotheses on the relationship between the language input quantities and the output quantity.

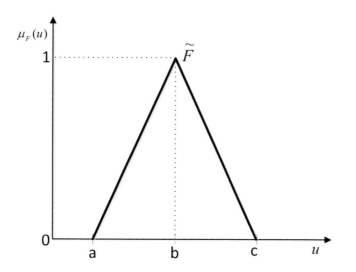

Figure 3. Triangular approximation of a membership function.

The rule-based language fuzzy model of the Mamdani type is given by the system $r = 1, 2, \ldots, R$ of the rules of the $IF - THEN$ type. Its r-th rule is in the form of the Mamdani-type rule [6]

IF [x_1 is $A_r(x_1)$ and x_2 is $A_r(x_2)$ and …and x_n is $A_r(x_n)$] $THEN$ [y is $B_r(y)$] .

The composite antecedent is composed of the fuzzy conjunction of partial fuzzy propositions of the size of the input variables; the consequent contains fuzzy propositions of the corresponding size of the output variable.

For the interpretation of the fuzzy logic conjunctions (fuzzy conjunction, fuzzy disjunction, fuzzy implications), variant forms can be used (t-norma function, t-conorma function, fuzzy implication function [8]).

To derive the fuzzy set size of the output variable, considering the specific values of the input varibles, the Mamdani deduction method is used. It assumes that among the antecedent propositions the fuzzy conjunction is interpreted as an ordinary conjunction (min), the fuzzy implication function THEN is interpreted as a Mamdani implication (min) and the individual rules are linked by a fuzzy disjunction interpreted as an ordinary disjunction (max). Let us consider the simple rule:

IF (X is A) $THEN$ (Y is B),

where A and B are fuzzy sets representing certain verbal values. The inference in the rule-based systems is based on the use of the Modus Ponens rule. In fuzzy systems, the generalized Fuzzy Modus Ponens rule [8] is used as follows:

assumption: (X is A')

condition: IF (X is A) $THEN$ (Y is B)

conclusion: (*Y is B'*).

If $A' = (U, \mu_{A'})$, then, the fuzzy set $B' = (V, \mu_{B'})$ can be determined as follows:

$$\mu_{B'}(y) = \max_{x \in U} \min\{\mu_{A'}(x), \mu_R(x, y)\},$$

where the universe U is the final set. It is actually the composition of the unary relation A' and the binary relation R. That is why we designate this way of reasoning as the compositional rule of inference [6].

Now, let us consider two fuzzy sets A and B defined on the universe U, described by their membership functions. The basic operations of their intersection $A \cap B$, union $A \cup B$ and unary operation of the complement A' can be expressed by standard relations:

$$\mu_{A \cap B}(x) = \min(\mu_A(x), \mu_B(x))$$

$$\mu_{A \cup B}(x) = \max(\mu_A(x), \mu_B(x))$$

$$\mu_{A'}(x) = 1 - \mu_A(x).$$

Fuzzy sets operations can be defined more generally. The class of operations which meet the conditions of the fuzzy intersection is called the class of operatios of the triangular t-norm, the class of operations which meet the conditions of the fuzzy union is called the class of operations of the triangular s-norm [6].

The IF-THEN rule expresses the causal relationship between the fuzzy propositions in the antecedent and consequent. This causal relationship represents a fuzzy relation which is represented by the fuzzy implication THEN. Again, unlike classic logic, the interpretation of fuzzy implication is not unambiguous (similarly as in the case of fuzzy conjunction, fuzzy disjunction, and fuzzy negation).

Let us consider that the basis of the expert system is composed of the Mamdani-type rules connected by the fuzzy logic operator *OR*, interpreted as a standard fuzzy disjunction (max, Gödel´s disjunction). Among the partial fuzzy statements of antecedents of the rules the fuzzy logic operator *AND* is used which is interpreted as a standard fuzzy conjunction (min, Gödel´s conjunction). Among the antecedents and consequents of the rules the fuzzy implication function *THEN* is used which is interpreted as standard fuzzy conjunction (min, Mamdani implication function).

The derivation of the form of the membership function of the output fuzzy set $B^0(y)$ is done by the Mamdani inferential method using the compositional rule of inference:

$$B^0(y) = R \circ A(x_j^0),$$

where $B^0(y)$ is the model input determined according to the general fuzzy model R, $\circ$ is the relation of the fuzzy composition and $A(x_j^0)$ is the vector of n- concrete values of input quantities, $j = 1, \ldots, n$. The form of the r-th rule of the Mamdani-type fuzzy model is:

IF [x_1 is $A_r(x_1)$ and x_2 is $A_r(x_2)$ and ...and x_n is $A_r(x_n)$] *THEN* [y is $B_r(y)$] .

The truth value of the j-th partial fuzzy proposition in the antecedent of the rule containing the j-th input variable x_{jin} in the r-th rule is calculated as fuzzy conjunction of particular fuzzy propositions in the antecedent of the rule interpreted as Gödel´s conjunction (minimum), i.e.,

$$\mu_{r,j} = \max \{ \min_{x_j} [A(x_j^0), A_r(x_j)] = Cons[A(x_j^0), A_r(x_j)] \}.$$

The output variable of the r-th rule is derived in the form of a fuzzy set with the membership function $B_r^0(y)$. It is calculated using the fuzzy implication function *THEN*, interpreted as the Mamdani implication function (minimum)

$$B_r^0(y) = \min_y \{ \mu_r, B_r(y) \} = \min_y \{ \min_j \{ [A(x_j^0), A_r(x_j)], B_r(y) \} \}.$$

The global output variable is then derived in the form of a fuzzy set with the membership function $B^0(y)$. It is calculated on condition of a fuzzy disjunctive connection of particular rules of the model when the fuzzy disjunction is interpreted as Gödel's disjunction (maximum)

$$B^0(y) = \max_y \{ B_r^0(y) \} = \max_y \{ \min_y \{ \min_j [A(x_j^0) \cup A_r(x_j)], B_r(y) \} \} \}.$$

To obtain the output value in the form of a crisp number y^{crisp}, the fuzzy set $B_r^0(y)$ is defuzzified by the relationship of the method COF (Center of Gravity)

$$y^{crisp} = \frac{\int_Y y \cdot \mu_{B_y} dy}{\int_Y \mu_{B_y} dy}$$

The fuzzy-logical approach is used for deduction in the programe system MATLAB [16] in which the implementation of the expert system is carried out - Subchapter 5.

2.3. Uncertainty Determination of Crisp Relations

Let us consider an ordinary analytic function with one output variable and the multidimensional argument:

$$y = f(\underline{s}, \underline{x}) \tag{2.4}$$

where $\underline{s}$ and $\underline{x}$ are vectors of its parameters and arguments defined as crisp real numbers. The corresponding uncertainty function is the modified expression (2.4), where $\underline{\tilde{s}}$ and $\underline{\tilde{x}}$ are vectors of its fuzzy parameters as fuzzy numbers, formalized and triangular fuzzy sets $\tilde{s}$ and $\tilde{x}$. The value of the dependent variable is then formalized as the fuzzy number $\tilde{y}$ - fuzzy set y. For example, a one-dimensional fuzzy function can be written in the form

$$\underline{\tilde{y}} = f(\underline{\tilde{s}}, \underline{\tilde{x}}).$$

To calculate the output value $\tilde{y}$, an algebra of fuzzy numbers has to be used [9]. The shape of fuzzy sets $\mu_{\tilde{B}}(y)$ as the result of any arithmetic operation f between fuzzy numbers $\mu(x_1),...,\mu(x_n)$ can be calculated according to the formula of Zadeh's extension principle:

$$\mu_{\tilde{B}}(y) = \begin{cases} \sup_{y=f(x_1,...,x_n)} \min\left[\mu(x_1),...,\mu(x_n)\right], & if\ \exists\, y = f(x_1,...,x_n) \\ 0\ else. \end{cases}$$

The Mamdani fuzzy rule-based models are used on the issue of choice of suppliers in the market environment (Subchapter 5).

The Mamdani fuzzy rule-based models are used to determine the size of the respondent's degree of fuzzy-belonging to the group and to fuzzify its evaluation. The synthesis of appropriate linguistic models is performed taking into account the consequences of expert´s hypotheses (Subchapter 6).

2.3.1. Fuzzy Arithmetics

The sense of fuzzy arithmetics is to define and perform equivalents of common arithmetic operations over fuzzified numbers [10]. As an example, let us take a simple addition of two numbers. If we add e.g., the numbers 2 + 5, the result is 7. If the numbers 2 and 5 were inaccurate, i.e., we were to add up "about 2" + "approximately 5," the result would be something like "about approximately 7."

The most frequently occurring expression of inaccuracy in the form of the above-mentioned attributes "about" or "approximately" can be expressed by means of a fuzzy set, the graph of which has the shape of a triangle – the so-called fuzzy number. With the increasing uncertainty of the value of the fuzzy number, the width of the base of this triangle increases. In Figure 4, we can see that the value $\tilde{A}_1$ is "about A," while the membership function from the point A, which is called the kernel, is to the left and to the right monotonously non-increasing.

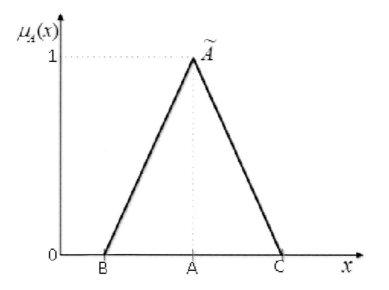

Figure 4. Fuzzy number "approximately A."

The extension principle defined by L. A. Zadeh in 1975 is the basis of fuzzy arithmetics. The conception of uncertainty is particularly advantageous because operations fuzzified in such a way transfer properties of both the numbers themselves and operations to the fuzzy environment. So if 2+5 is 7, then "about 2" + "about 5" is just "about approximately 7." By the vague term "about approximately," we express that both inaccuracies from the two addends will appear together in the resulting sum. The sum of two inaccurate numbers is therefore always less accurate than either of these two numbers. For some other fuzzified operations (e.g., multiplication), the inaccuracy of the result is even greater than the sum of the individual inaccuracies of the operands.

The extension principle applied to our case of the binary operation over real numbers looks as follows:

$$\widetilde{+}(\tilde{X}, \tilde{Y})(z) = \bigvee_{\forall x \in X, \forall y \in Y:\ x+y=z} \min(\tilde{X}(x), \tilde{Y}(y)) .$$

Of course, this formula can be simply generalized also to arbitrary n-ary operations.

The used method of computer implementation of fuzzy arithmetics uses the α-cut method [26]. The algorithm of α-cuts proceeds as follows: First, we divide the set L into discrete elements. These will be evenly distributed within the interval L, i.e., for N elements, we will select the step $\frac{1}{N-1}$ and we will watch out for numerical errors so that the last element is not just below or just above 1, but exactly 1. Each value from such a discrete set L will be called the α-level. Since we work with fuzzy numbers and not with general fuzzy sets, each fuzzy number can now be represented by means of N pairs of numbers because for each α-level, we just need to remember the smallest and largest value of the universe where the membership degree is greater or equal to the particular α value

$$\tilde{X}: \{\forall \alpha \in L: \{\min x, \max x\}_\alpha: \tilde{X}(x) \geq \alpha\}.$$

If we have the operands converted into such a form of α-cuts, then, also the calculation of the fuzzy operation itself can be performed directly over the α-cuts. To find the resulting interval at the given alpha-level, it is sufficient to calculate the given operation above the intervals of operands at the same alpha-level only. If this calculation is implemented separately for particular concrete binary operations, it can usually be simplified down to a calculation with numbers only $\{\min x, \max x\}$ expressing the boundaries of the intervals of the α-cuts of the operands. The calculation is always performed separately for each alpha-level.

Now, let us have a look at the implementation of particular operations at a certain alpha-level. Let us assume this form of the general binary operation $\otimes$:

$$\tilde{V} = \tilde{X} \otimes \tilde{Y}$$

For each alpha-level, we look for the left and right boundary of the interval (L and R indices):

$$\{V_L, V_R\} = \{X_L, X_R\} \otimes \{Y_L, Y_R\}$$

The formulas discussed below are valid also for the combination of fuzzy numbers and real numbers. The sum is the easiest operation, it is sufficient to add the left and right boundaries of the intervals

$$V_L = X_L + Y_L$$

$$V_R = X_R + Y_R .$$

As to the difference, we always deduct from each boundary of the first operand the opposite boundary of the second operand:

$$V_L = X_L - Y_R$$

$$V_R = X_R - .Y_L.$$

For the product, a formula similar to the sum applies:

$$V_L = X_L \cdot Y_L$$

$$V_R = X_R \cdot Y_R.$$

A formula similar to the difference applies to the share:

$$V_L = X_L / Y_R$$

$$V_R = X_R / Y_L.$$

The real power of the fuzzy number in the form $\tilde{X}^y$ where $y \in \mathbb{R}$ can be calculated as follows:

$$V_L = \left(X_L\right)^y$$

$$V_R = \left(X_R\right)^y$$

The square root of the fuzzy number is considered for the positive part of the universe only (applies to the operand as well as the result of the operation), i.e., $\tilde{V}, \tilde{X}: \mathbb{R}^{0+} \rightarrow L$. We can calculate it as follows:

$$V_L = \sqrt{X_L}$$

$$V_R = \sqrt{X_R}$$

The created software FAv1.00 [11] is designed as a programmable user application. Figure 5 shows its main window where, on the left, we can see the entered computational program, the rest of the window is filled by graphs of particular calculated results.

The analysis has shown that the method or algorithm based on α-cuts achieves very good results in terms of velocity, as it is only linearly dependent on the number of cuts performed over the interval [0,1]. At the same time, it shows a very good accuracy.

The fuzzy arithmetics formulas are used to carry out the fuzzy relationship in Subchapter 6.

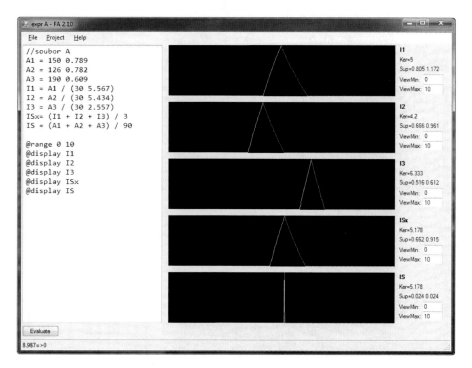

Figure 5. Main windows of the FAv1.00 application.

3. PROBABISTICALLY ORIENTED TECHNOLOGY OF AN EXPERT SYSTEM

The technology utilizing the pseudo-Bayesian principles deals with the synthesis of the abstract model of the expert system for determining the level of corporate social responsibility of an enterprise (CSR). The language rule-based modelling and the inference method are based on the pseudo-Bayesian approach [4]. The presented expert system is a relevant module of the built hierarchical structure aimed at the research of impacts of activities of economic entities on the social system.

Economic entities influence the society and more or less contribute to the development and growth of the people´s living standard. However, it is difficult to define completely and precisely all activities which have an influence on the social system. This fact is influenced by two circumstances – the dynamics of the social system and its uncertainty. The social system is currently constantly changing and economic entities have to respond to these changes, change their activities, and adapt to the surrounding influences. The complexity of its structures and a strong uncertainty of its behaviour, conditioned by the inclusion of the human factor, are typical features of the social system. It is characterized by lack of accurate measured data and accurate information about its behaviour.

The chapter introduces a design of a program computer system which through abstract models comprehensively and objectively evaluates the impact of activities of business subjects on social environment in which they are included.

The determination of the influence of the production and non-production activities of economic entities on social environment is carried out by gradual inclusion of particular evaluation aspects into the evaluation modules for the determination of partial effects as aspects for the determination of the final effects. This method enables the use of a hierarchical computational structure, in which partial levels represent modules for determining partial effects as aggregate aspects (inputs) for the following hierarchical level. This solution provides a number of advantages, in particular, the division of the whole system into subsystems (modules) – simplification of the design and tuning of the transformation models – openness of the system – the possibility of adding additional modules in case of the expansion of the task.

The system model is not only a comprehensive system including a number of difficultly mathematically defined functions and linkages but also – due to the significant inclusion of the human factor – a typical vague system. The transformation of input aspects (input variable modules) into output effects (output variable modules) is carried out by expert systems. Rule-based language models are their core; transformation algorithms are based on the principles of unconventional probabilities.

Numerical (data) input aspects (input variables) of the module of each hierarchical level can be directly measurable or calculated as evaluation criteria y in the blocks of the data preparation

$$y = f(x_1,...,x_m).$$

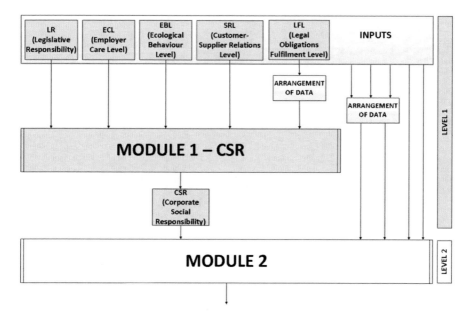

Figure 6. General scheme of the hierarchical system.

Language models enable quantification of (uncertain) input variables either by means of language quantifiers of the "little, moderately, a lot of" type (fuzzy-logical models), or expert evaluation of the current numerical input values by probability degrees (probability models). The system contains fuzzy-stochastic computational blocks, enabling mutual exchange of information between the two types of models.

Figure 6 presents a general scheme of the proposed hierarchical system for the determination of impacts of activities of economic entities on the society. The sections highlighted in colour represent the functions of the first level of deduction. This is namely the probabilistic Module 1 – CSR which is designed to determine the level of corporate social responsibility of a company [12] – see Figure 6.

In the probabilistic module MODULE 1-CSR for the investigation of impacts of activities in the area of CSR, the behaviour of economic entities is evaluated from four perspectives. There are three main responsibilities of a company – pillars (social pillar, economic pillar, and ecological pillar), to which we added the legal responsibility [13]. We consider the compliance with legal obligations the essential parameter of an organization, as we assume that if an organization does not comply with applicable laws, it is not socially responsible [13, 14, 15].

We will calculate (deduce) the level of social responsibility of companies on the basis of four company activities (four input language variables in the model). Input variables are namely

- employees care level ECL
- ecological behaviour level EBL
- customer-supplier relations level SRL
- legal obligations fulfilment level LFL
- legislative responsibility LR

The language values of output variable determine the extent to which the company is socially responsible or not. Output variable of the module

- corporate social responsibility CSR – has the following language values: None - Low – Satisfactory – Good – Excellent.

In the described model, knowledge is represented by means of the IF-THEN rules in the form of

$IF \langle premise\,E \rangle \; THEN \; \langle conclusion\,H \rangle \; WITH\langle probabilit\!\!\!\;\!\!y\; P(H\,|\,E)\rangle$

$ELSE \langle conclusion\,H \rangle \; WITH\langle probabilit\!\!\!\;\!\!y\; P(H\,|\,not\,E)\rangle$,

where the values $P(H\,|\,E)$ and $P(H\,|\,not\,E)$ are entered by the expert.

The set of these rules forms an oriented graph in which the vertices represent the propositions (E, H) and the edges evaluated by probabilities form the rules. This graph aims to represent the knowledge being processed during the inference process and is called the inference network (Figure 7). The propositions which always represent premises are the leaves in the graph (input variables). On the contrary, the conclusions assume the position of the graph roots (root nodes – output variables). Other propositions are intermediate propositions and can represent both partial conclusions and premises. These are logical combinations of propositions in the forms of *not E*, E_1 and E_2, E_1 or E_2. Therefore, two types of nodes can be distinguished – the Bayesian node and logical node [5].

The Bayesian node represents a proposition, the probability of which can be evaluated on the basis of the Bayes' theorem. It has a given prior probability. Posterior probability is determined based on observed premises or is acquired by direct observation. Bayesian nodes are the input variables of the model.

Logical node represents the proposition, the probability of which can be evaluated based on a logical combination of premises. The proposition probability is evaluated with the use of relations adopted from fuzzy logic (2.3.)

$$P\!\left(E_1\;\&\;E_2\right) = \min\!\left\{P(E_1), P(E_2)\right\}$$

$$P\!\left(E_1 \vee E_2\right) = \max\!\left\{P(E_1), P(E_2)\right\}$$

$$P(not\,E) = 1 - P(E) \,.$$

The CSR model contains four logical nodes:

- SOCIAL (Social Responsibility) – ECL and LFL
- ECOLOGICAL (Ecological Responsibility) – EBL and LFL
- ECONOMIC (Economic Responsibility) – SRL and LFL
- BLR (Breach of Legislative Responsibility) – not LR

A company is not legally liable (BLR node), if it doesn´t comply with the legal obligations associated with the activity of the particular legal entity (not LR). The legal obligations include legislation of a given type of organization, such as proper publication of information about the organization as defined by law, corruption-free behaviour, proper fulfilment of tax obligations, and legislation of individual pillars, such as observance of the Labour Code, observance of the legal obligations in the field of ecology [15]. Compliance with legal obligations or overall legislative responsibility (LR variable) is considered the essential observed parameter of an organization, as the initial premise is that if an organization does not comply with the valid legislation, it is not socially responsible.

An organization is socially responsible (SOCIAL node), if it complies with the law in the field (LFL variable) and, in addition, takes care of its employees, invests in their education and above-standard working conditions, evaluates observance of equal opportunities and human rights, is interested in the balance of work and private life of employees, enables employees to get involved in social activities and thereby supports mutual solidarity of people in the region where it is based, and promotes the policy called Good Corporate Citizenship (ECL variable) [15].

An organization is ecologically responsible (ECOLOGICAL node), if it complies with the environmental legislation (LFL variable) and, in addition, it behaves ecologically even beyond its legal obligations to reduce its environmental impact, invests in ecological activities, invests in technologies which demonstrably save energy and natural resources (EBL variable) [15].

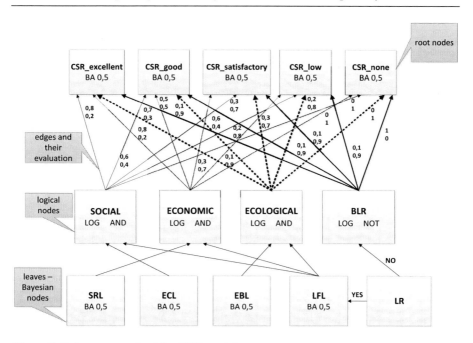

Figure 7. Inference graph of the CSR model.

An organization is economically responsible (ECONOMIC node), if it complies with the law in the field (LFL variable) and, in addition, it also e.g., actively demonstrates its corruption-free behaviour and publishes more information than is its statutory duty, makes fair supplier-customer relationships (SRL variable), i.e., a quality product for the customer, maximum services for the customer´s advantage, prefers local suppliers, selects business partners based on the approach to employees and the environment, cares for the customer life quality, has a fair approach to the competitors, etc. [15].

Uncertainty is expressed by the probability value. However, it is not a mathematical probability, but a subjective probability which is entered by the expert, therefore the term pseudo-probability is often used for it.

Two subjective probabilities P(H | E) and P(H | not E) entered by the expert which are the numerical parameters from the interval ⟨0;1⟩ are matched to each rule. Through this evaluation we express the uncertainty of the rule, e.g.,

IF <*E₁*: A company is economically responsible> *THEN* <*H*: CSR is excellent> *WITH* <$P(H \mid E_1) = 0{,}8$; $P(H \mid not\ E_1) = 0{,}2$>

IF <*E₂*: A company is socially responsible> *THEN* <*H*: CSR is good> *WITH* <$P(H \mid E_2) = 0{,}6$; $P(H \mid not\ E_2) = 0{,}4$>

IF <*E₃*: A company is ecologically responsible> *THEN* <*H*: CSR is low> *WITH* <$P(H \mid E_3) = 0{,}2$; $P(H \mid not\ E_3) = 0{,}8$>.

To create the model, we used the system FEL EX Expert. Its methods and the way of processing uncertainty are based on the prospector model [5].

We will verify the correctness of the model by simulation experiments. Simulation calculations are performed as follows – as model inputs, we assign numerical values of the input variables – the subjective probability level of the rule premises and the model derives the corresponding confidence values of the target hypotheses (corporate social responsibility levels). Numeric values of input variables and the output variable values are shown in Table 1.

Table 1. Input variables values of simulations 1 - 4

Simulation	Input variables					Output variable				
	LR	LFL	SRL	ECL	EBL	CSR_ none	CSR_ low	CSR_ satisfactory	CSR_ good	CSR_ excellent
1	yes	0,8	0,6	0,7	0,5	0,00	0,80	0,85	0,91	0,95
2	yes	0,3	0,4	0,1	0,2	0,00	0,99	0,98	0,84	0,54
3	no	-	0,6	0,8	0,7	0,99	0,10	0,10	0,10	0,10
4	yes	1	0,3	0,2	0,2	0,00	0,99	0,97	0,85	0,61

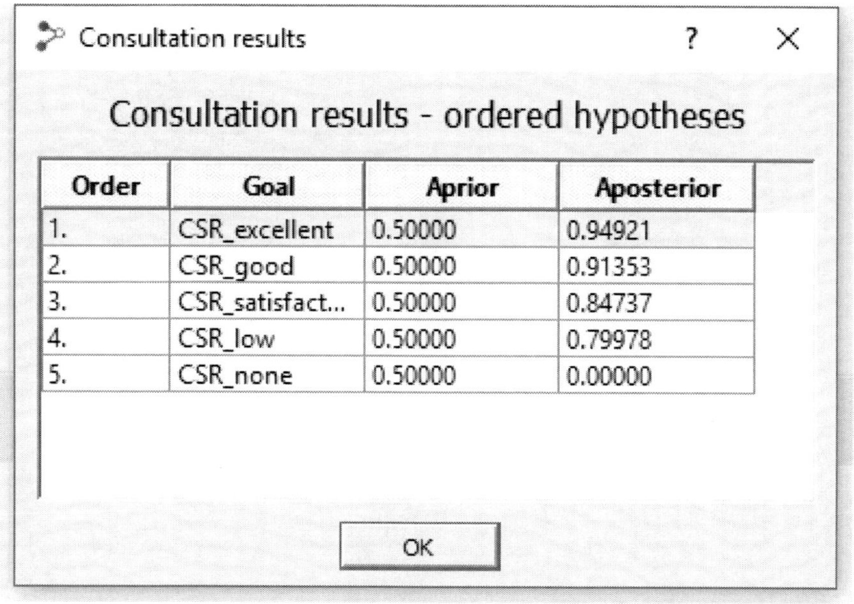

Consultation results

Consultation results - ordered hypotheses

Order	Goal	Aprior	Aposterior
1.	CSR_excellent	0.50000	0.94921
2.	CSR_good	0.50000	0.91353
3.	CSR_satisfact...	0.50000	0.84737
4.	CSR_low	0.50000	0.79978
5.	CSR_none	0.50000	0.00000

OK

Figure 8. 1st simulation results.

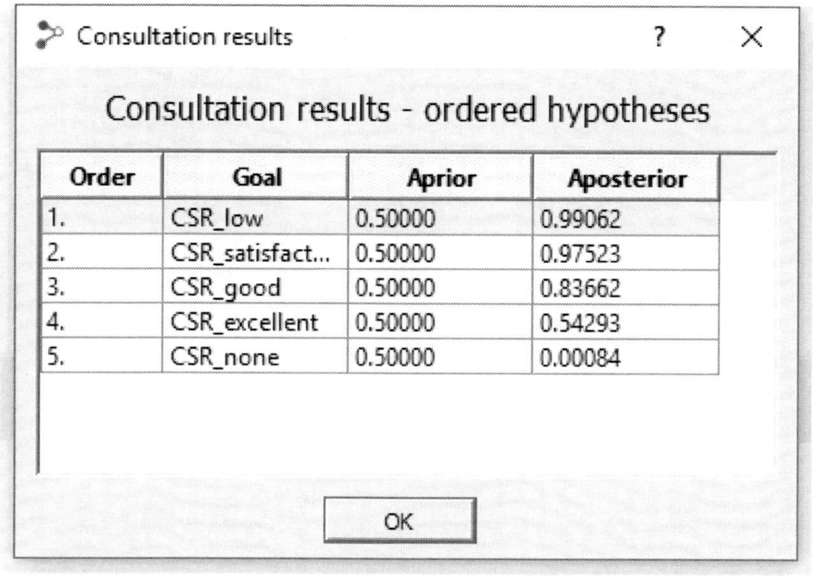

Consultation results

Consultation results - ordered hypotheses

Order	Goal	Aprior	Aposterior
1.	CSR_low	0.50000	0.99062
2.	CSR_satisfact...	0.50000	0.97523
3.	CSR_good	0.50000	0.83662
4.	CSR_excellent	0.50000	0.54293
5.	CSR_none	0.50000	0.00084

OK

Figure 9. 2nd simulation results.

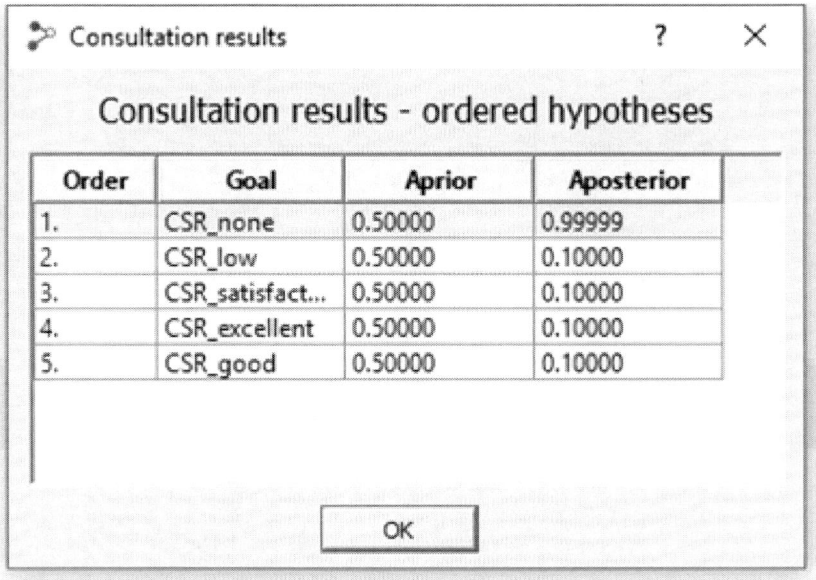

Consultation results   ?   ✕

Consultation results - ordered hypotheses

Order	Goal	Aprior	Aposterior
1.	CSR_none	0.50000	0.99999
2.	CSR_low	0.50000	0.10000
3.	CSR_satisfact...	0.50000	0.10000
4.	CSR_excellent	0.50000	0.10000
5.	CSR_good	0.50000	0.10000

OK

Figure 10. 3rd simulation results.

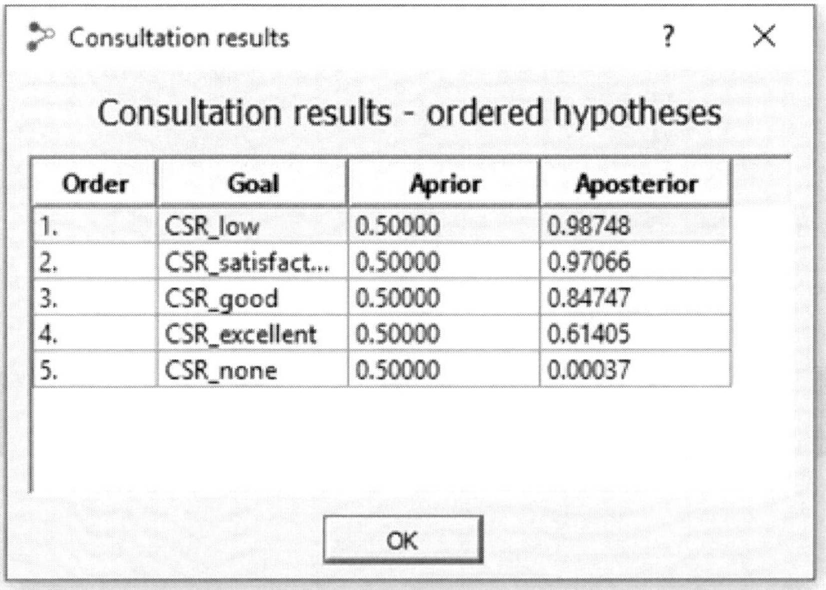

Consultation results   ?   ✕

Consultation results - ordered hypotheses

Order	Goal	Aprior	Aposterior
1.	CSR_low	0.50000	0.98748
2.	CSR_satisfact...	0.50000	0.97066
3.	CSR_good	0.50000	0.84747
4.	CSR_excellent	0.50000	0.61405
5.	CSR_none	0.50000	0.00037

OK

Figure 11. 4th simulation results.

The third simulation (see Table 1, Figure 10) shows a situation in which a company fails to fulfil its legal obligations and, in this simulated situation, it also violates them in a punishable way and although in other activities it manifests a rather intense activity, it is not socially responsible.

The last simulation shows a company which, on the contrary, totally complies with the legal obligations and also with those that are not enforceable but its remaining activities are rather random actions. In this case, the company is socially responsible, but its social responsibility is rather low or almost satisfactory (see Table 1, Figure 11).

Comparing the results, it is clear that a company which does not accurately approach the legal obligations and has an elaborated, responsible approach to its customers, employees as well as the environment is significantly more socially responsible than a company which fully accurately approaches legal obligations, yet, at the same time, has an apathetic approach to its internal and external environment. A company acting illegally can not redeem through its activities towards internal or external environment its illegality and thus is not socially responsible. On the other hand, a company paying at least partial attention to all its duties as well as its environment is socially responsible, albeit only on a low or satisfactory level.

The simulation experiments have shown that the proposed model produces the right results. However, the functionality of the model will still need to be verified in practice.

4. FUZZY-LOGIC ORIENTED EXPERT SYSTEM TECHNOLOGY

The technology utilizing the fuzzy-logical principles focuses on the issue of choice of suppliers in the market environment. The global decision-making task is split into partial tasks; the expert modules are integrated into a 5-level hierarchical structure for their formalization. The chapter presents the structures of constituent language models and implementation of the structure of expert systems in the MATLAB-Simulink program environment [16]. The efficiency of the decision-making system is proven by the solution of a simulation exercise. Economic entities as integral parts of the social system have an impact on it. The complexity of structures and uncertainty of behaviour which are also conditioned by incorporating the human factor are the typical characteristics of economic entities and the social system.

In the last decades the area of computer support of decision-making tasks has seen a significant leap forward. One of the modern trends is also the implementation of unconventional methods of artificial intelligence (neural networks, fuzzy mathematics, expert systems) [17, 18]. The methods are based on the implementation of knowledge of skilled experts. This knowledge thus creates the basis for their high quality knowledge mental models. Knowledge language models of expert systems are then created to formalize these mental models in computing. The usage of expert systems has, in the task of supplier choice solution, a considerable potential [19, 20].

The main aim of this paper is to analyse the decision-making task of the supplier choice, leading to the particular sub-tasks and the proposal of the corresponding language models of expert systems. Further aims are the presentation of the current trends in the field of expert system implementation in supplier choice evaluation, presentation of principles and procedures of the synthesis of fuzzy oriented expert systems for the solution of partial sub-tasks, integration of a global hierarchical expert system, simulation verification of the function of the system on the example of choice of two existing and two new suppliers, results analysis and the outlook on the direction of further research.

The general model of the solved problem (knowledge base) is not mathematical, but language-based. The *IF-THEN* rule statements are used to formulate the conditional statements that describe the behaviour of the system under modelling. For example the rule expresses the linguistic dependency of the linguistic output variable Supplier Quality (SUQ) on two input linguistic variables, namely Processes Quality (PRQ) and Product Quality (PQA). This is linguistically expressed in the form:

If process quality is high and product quality is sufficient, then supplier's quality is average.

Then, the corresponding rule has the form:

IF (PRQ is HIGH) and (PQA is SUFFICIENT) THEN (SUQ is AVERAGE).

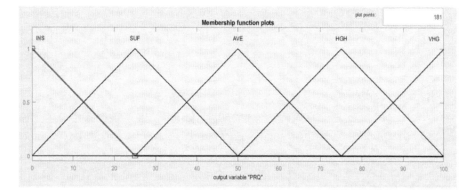

Figure 12. Output variable PRQ – fuzzy sets of linguistic terms in MATLAB.

The linguistic values of the input/output linguistic variables are expressed using linguistic terms. The linguistic terms are represented as fuzzy sets. For example, the linguistic values of the output variable PRQ are defined as: "Insufficient (INS), Sufficient (SUF), Average (AVE), High (HGH), Very High (VGH)." Their membership functions are expressed using a broken-line triangular approximation (programe system MATLAB – Figure 12).

The suggested hierarchic expert system contains eight partial expert systems, the language models of which (knowledge base) are based on the above-mentioned principles.

The proposed supplier suitability evaluation using the decision-making expert system is of a hierarchical type and is diversified into 4 partial decision-making levels with 8 partial decision-making blocks ES1-1 to ES 4-1 (Figure 13).

According to the authors [21, 22, 23], the basic indicators of supplier suitability are as follows: Quality (ES 3-1), Total cost (3-2), Delivery terms (ES 3-3) and Supplier flexibility (ES 3-4). The suggested new method investigates quality from two points of view – Processes quality (ES 2-1) and Product quality (ES 2-2). Processes quality in the supplier company can be described from the following aspects: Processes Audit Results (ES 1-1), Product Certification (ISO), Time on the market and References. The processes audit should be done by a representative of the customer company. The evaluation in this system is fully dependent on the opinion of the expert. The audit proceeds according to the following categories: Communication, Quality control, Technological development, Clean production application. The evaluation according to the mentioned parameters enables a complex examination of the suitability of the particular applicants. The product quality can be examined from two points of view: Compulsory product certification, Processes quality control. The processes quality is evaluated in the course of the control according to the opinion of the expert.

ES 3-2: Total costs: Purchasing value, Transport costs, Costs of packaging, Costs of storage, Costs tariff. The costs are examined separately. This is therefore also the potential improvement – the examination of total costs.

ES 3-3: Delivery terms: Distance to supplier, Delivery time. The authors see these two parameters as interconnected.

ES 3-4 Supplier flexibility: Possibility of online orders, Possibility of product modification, Possibility of joint development, Possibility of activities delegation, Possibility of deferred payment. This is one of the most important groups in the evaluation. The answers are formulated in the form of both yes-no answers and the scale of absolute absence through absolute presence of the service.

The partial expert systems ES 1-1 to ES 4-1 are integrated in the hierarchical structure outlined in Figure 4. Their relations result from the logical sequence of the need for a solution of the specific sub-tasks.

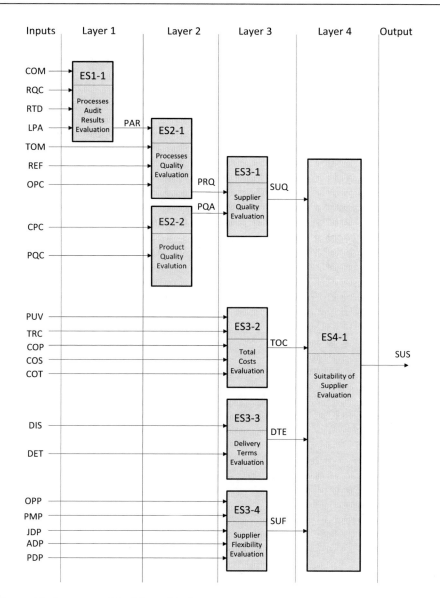

Figure 13. Structure of the hierarchical expert system.

ES 4-1 Suitability of supplier – final evaluation of the suppliers is done from the point of view of total costs, delivery terms and supplier flexibility. The supplier is evaluated on the scale from 0 to 100.

Table 2. Expert System Linguistic input/output variables

Name of variable	IDENT
Communication	COM
Results of quality control	RQC
Rate of technological development	RTD
Lean production application	LPA
Processes audit results	VAP
References	REF
Time of market	OPC
Processes quality	KPC
Compulsory product certification	CPC
Results of processes quality control	PQC
Product quality	PRQ
Quality	PQA
Purchasing value	PUV
Transport costs	TRC
Costs of packaging	COP
Costs of storage	COS
Costs tariff	COT
Total costs	TOC
Distance to supplier	DIS
Delivery time	DET
Delivery terms	DTE
Possibility of online orders	OPP
Possibility of product modification	PMP
Possibility of joint development	JDP
Possibility of activities delegation	ADP
Possibility of deferred payment	PDP
Supplier flexibility	SUF
Sustainability of supplier	SUS

Table 3. Simulation experiments results

SupplieR 1 Large Local Producer					Supplier 2 Large Foreign Producer					Supplier 3 Large Distributor					Supplier 4 Small Distributor				
ESM	Exp	Syst	e	%	ESM	Exp	Sys	e	%	ESM	Exp	Syst	e	%	ESM	Exp	Syst	e	%
ES 1-1	65-75	73	0	0	ES 1-1	65-70	79	9	13	ES 1-1	65-75	68	0	0	ES 1-1	65-70	78	8	11
ES 2-1	50-60	50	0	0	ES 2-1	20-25	23	0	0	ES 2-1	20-30	20	0	0	ES 2-1	10-15	19	4	27
ES 2-2	80	75	5	6	ES 2-2	55	53	2	4	ES 2-2	80	75	5	6	ES 2-2	50-55	53	0	0
ES 3-1	65-70	75	5	7	ES 3-1	30-35	28	2	7	ES 3-1	20-30	24	0	0	ES 3-1	5-10	9	0	0
ES 3-2	25-35	31	0	0	ES 3-2	45-55	42	3	7	ES 3-2	65-75	60	5	8	ES 3-2	65-75	59	6	9
ES 3-3	80-90	91	1	1	ES 3-3	25-30	33	3	10	ES 3-3	65-70	74	4	6	ES 3-3	65-75	76	1	1
ES 3-4	65-75	75	0	0	ES 3-4	45-55	60	5	9	ES 3-4	10-15	8	2	13	ES 3-4	10-15	8	2	13
ES 4-1	85-95	90	0	0	ES 4-1	50-55	60	5	9	ES 4-1	25-30	34	4	13	ES 4-1	25-30	34	4	13

The input/output linguistic variables are defined by an expert. Their overview and the expert system classification is noted in Table 2.

The partial expert systems ES 1-1 to ES 4-1 were implemented in the software development environment Fuzzy ToolBox of the MATLAB program package. Their simulation hierarchical structure was created in the Simulink (MATLAB) environment [16].

A common comparison of new and current suppliers is important in the current age. The crucial issue is the simultaneous comparison of factual and estimated values – such an important factor is also the complexity of the decision-making task, represented by the complexity (the number of rules) of its language model.

The correctness of the function of the expert system is evaluated by the absolute difference between the expert's estimation and the expert system's estimation (Table 3). The level of the presented system shows the absolute error of the specific modules in the range of 0 - 27%. The worst accuracy of 27% is shown in one out of four inferences of the system ES 2-1, and yet, in all three other cases, the error is zero. This situation is typical for the request of fine tuning of its language model. The other cases show the margin of error of 0 – 13%. The same margin of error was shown by the resulting inference of ES 4–1. It means absolute error is 8.7%. It can be said that according to the practical experience from the field of knowledge engineering, an estimation error of up to 10% is acceptable.

5. FUZZY-STATISTICALLY ORIENTED EXPERT SYSTEM TECHNOLOGY

The technology utilizing the fuzzy approaches and mathematical models principles is focused on dealing with the fact that methods of calculating indicators and standards of quality of the outputs of the systems involving the human factor do not take into account the substantial property of the processed data – their natural uncertainty. Data, which have their origin in the human evaluation of phenomena using the integer numerical values, are a typical example of such a vagueness of overloaded information. Unconventional methods of soft-computing are able to complete numeric information with the degree of its uncertainty as well. In the chapter, these approaches are applied to determine the certain performance indicator in the frame of Balanced Scorecard [24] by means of fuzzification of the input figures of respondents with their subsequent processing by means of fuzzy arithmetic and fuzzy-logic [25]. Crisp numbers are replaced with fuzzy numbers; their uncertainty is determined by using four fuzzy-logic expert subsystems. Rule-based knowledge bases are based on the expert hypotheses which can be expressed as the relation between the uncertainty of the respondent's respond and his mental characteristics and attitudes. Expert systems are implemented both in the FEL-Expert program and in the fuzzy arithmetic software system. The uncertainty of the resulting criteria creates new information which leads to improving the efficiency of their use in decision-making processes.

Using the fuzzy approach to formalize vague phenomena is a method which belongs to the artificial intelligence area. The chapter links vagueness with the Balanced Scorecard (BSC) and shows both the benefit for managerial decision-making and methodology of how to formalize the vagueness of evaluation criteria using fuzzy rule models. Simulations are used to verify the efficiency. This is needed as common tools are obsolete and performance is in vague areas.

Customer satisfaction index (CSI) is usually discovered by means of a statistical survey, while using scaled answers [26]. As an example we can take a classification of customer satisfaction with certain products when we evaluate answers using the whole numbers lying in the interval $< 0,10 >$ (0 means unsatisfied, 10 satisfied).

As supplementary information, we ask for classification into groups which is the multiple choice question distinguishing 1 – "I concentrate on new products and I am willing to pay for distinct products," 2 – "I buy regular products for regular price" and 3 – "I buy products on sale for low prices."

Let us assume the answers from the customers might not be definite, as each customer perceives the scale differently. The same level of satisfaction can lead different respondents to various answers. Also the respondent is not able to transform the whole width of approaches, feelings, etc. into one precise number and the sharp value of the scale.

We have to expect that two identically feeling respondents will not mark the same value of the offered scale and, at the same time, a respondent when asked repeatedly will choose an answer different from the one he marked before.

Conventional mathematical model for the determination of partial and global evaluation criteria is given by this relation

$$IS_h = \frac{1}{K_h} \sum_{j=1}^{K_h} A_{j,h} \qquad (5.1)$$

where $A_{j,h}$ is the answer of the respondent j in the group h and K_h is the total number of respondents in the group h. The global customer satisfaction index is expressed as

$$IS = \frac{1}{K} \sum_{j=1}^{K} A_j \qquad (5.2)$$

where K is the total number of respondents and A_j is a value of the answer of the respondent j from the total number of respondents.

Since we assume that the respondents' answers are affected by vagueness, we will continue with the process of determination how to express this vagueness and how to incorporate it into our consideration.

5.1. Fuzzification of the Respondent's Group Belonging

Crisp belonging of the respondent j to the group h (respondent included into the group as *"exactly 1"*) is as follows

$$k_{j,h}^{NAL} = 1 . \qquad (5.3)$$

Uncertain belonging (respondent j included into the group as *"approximately 1"*) is

$$\tilde{k}_{j,h}^{NAL} = \tilde{1} \text{ "approximately 1."} \tag{5.4}$$

The uncertainty of belonging of the respondent j ($j = 1,2,...,K_h$) to the group h (h = 1, 2, 3) is formalized by a triangular fuzzy number $\tilde{k}_{j,h}^{NAL}$, Figure 14.

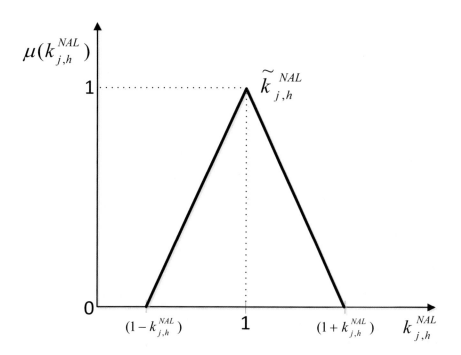

Figure 14. Fuzzy Numbers of the Amount.

In case of zero uncertainty then (5.3) is applicable, in case of uncertainty, belonging of a respondent to a group is given by a fuzzy number (5.4).

According to Figure 14, the fuzzy number $\tilde{k}_{j,h} \equiv \tilde{1}$ is its core "1" (Ker) and two partial fuzzy intervals $\left(\Delta_L \tilde{k}_{j,h}^{NAL}, \Delta_P \tilde{k}_{j,h}^{NAL}\right)$ are defined as follows

$$\widetilde{k}_{j,h}\left\{\left[\left(1-k_{j,h}^{NAL}\right)\right],1,\left[\left(1+k_{j,h}^{NAL}\right)\right]\right\}=\widetilde{k}_{j,h}\left\{\left[\left(\Delta_L\widetilde{k}_{j,h}^{NAL}\right)\right],1,\left[\left(\Delta_P\widetilde{k}_{j,h}^{NAL}\right)\right]\right\}.$$

The rate of uncertainty $\widetilde{k}_{j,h}^{NAL}$, Fig. 2, is given by a fuzzy model for each respondent separately considering the hypotheses and according to his evaluation of satisfaction $A_{j,h}$. The value of $k_{j,h}^{NAL}$ represents the contribution from all the involved hypotheses.

The respondent is then included in the amount of respondents in the group h as a sum of the fuzzy units

$$\widetilde{k}_h^{NAL}=\sum_{j=1}^{K_h}\widetilde{1}_{j,h}$$

where K_h is a sharp number of respondents in the group h, $h = 1, 2, 3$.

5.2. Fuzzification of the Respondent's Evaluation

The fuzzified value of the evaluation of satisfaction of the respondent j in the group h marked with the symbol $A_{j,h}$ is expressed by a fuzzy number $\widetilde{A}_{j,h}$ according to Figure 15.

The rate of the evaluation uncertainty $k_{j,h}^{HOD}$ of the respondent j from the group h is calculated using the fuzzy model considering the contributions of uncertainty rates of the hypotheses considered. The triangular fuzzy number $\widetilde{A}_{j,h}$ is defined as follows

$$\widetilde{A}_{j,h}=\left\{\left[\left(A_{j,h}-k_{j,h}^{HOD}\right)\right],A_{j,h},\left[\left(A_{j,h}+k_{j,h}^{HOD}\right)\right]\right\}. \tag{5.5}$$

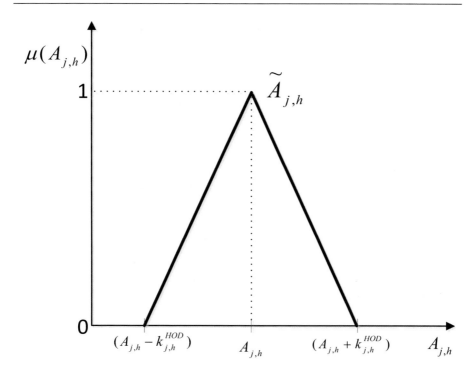

Figure 15. Fuzzy Numbers of the Evaluation of Respondents.

The index of customer satisfaction of the group h is a triangular fuzzy number $\widetilde{IS}_h$, formalized by a fuzzy set with a triangular membership function

$$\widetilde{IS}_h \left\{ \left[IS_h - k_{j,h}^{HOD} \right], IS_h, \left[IS_h + k_{j,h}^{HOD} \right] \right\} = IS_h \left\{ \left[\Delta_L \widetilde{IS}_h \right], IS_{h,} \left[\Delta_P \widetilde{IS}_h \right] \right\}.$$

The rate of index uncertainty IS_h is given by the sum of the left and right indeterminate intervals

$$\Delta \widetilde{IS}_h = \Delta_L \widetilde{IS}_h + \Delta_P \widetilde{IS}_h \ .$$

The global index of customer satisfaction is also a triangular fuzzy number $\widetilde{IS}$, formalized by a fuzzy set with a triangular membership function

$$\widetilde{IS}\left\{\left[\left(IS-k_{j}\right)\right],IS,\left[\left(IS+k_{j}\right)\right]\right\}=IS\left\{\left[\left(\Delta_{L}\widetilde{IS}\right)\right],IS,\left[\left(\Delta_{P}\widetilde{IS}\right)\right]\right\}.$$

The rate of index uncertainty $\widetilde{IS}$ is given by the sum of the left and right indeterminate intervals

$$\Delta\,\widetilde{IS}=\Delta_{L}\widetilde{IS}+\Delta_{P}\widetilde{IS}\;.$$

To evaluate the rate of index uncertainty, we have possibility to compare results of two statistical surveys A and B (see Table 4).

5.3. Fuzzification of Evaluation Indices

The fuzzified index of customer satisfaction within groups (5.1) is now given by the relationship of the fuzzy multiplication of the sum of fuzzy numbers

$$\widetilde{IS}_{h}=\frac{1}{\widetilde{K}_{h}}\sum_{j=1}^{K_{h}}\widetilde{A}_{j,h}\;,\quad h=1,2,3\;.$$

The global fuzzified index of customer satisfaction (5.2) is now given by

$$\widetilde{IS}=\frac{1}{\widetilde{K}}\sum_{j=1}^{K}\widetilde{A}_{j}$$

where $\widetilde{A}_{j}$ is a fuzzified evaluation of the respondent j and K is the total number of respondents.

The values k_j^{HOD}, k_h^{HOD} (see 6.5) and k are defined by fuzzy models. The calculation of the fuzzy relationships is carried out with the help of fuzzy arithmetic.

To quantify the uncertainty of the correctness of respondents' answers, we define 4 expert fuzzy-logical rules, formalizing the existing facts (evidence) and their impacts (hypotheses) in the form $E \rightarrow H$. The relations for estimating the uncertainty of customer satisfaction indices as fuzzy numbers are also expressed.

1. Customers overestimate themselves (include themselves in a higher group) → the number of customers in the group $h = 1$ and $h = 2$ is excessive. The uncertainty of the respondent's belonging to groups $h = 1$ and $h = 2$ is the higher, the higher or lower the level of its evaluation is. The uncertainty of the respondent's belonging to group $h = 3$ is low.

2. Exhibitionists are included in the set (in the group $h = 1$, there are more positive exhibitionists, in the group $h = 3$, there are more negative exhibitionists) → the amount of customers in the groups 1 and 3 is excessive. The uncertainty of the respondent's belonging to the group $h = 1$ is the higher, the higher the level of his evaluation is. The uncertainty of the respondent's belonging to the group $h = 3$ is the higher, the lower the level of his evaluation is. The uncertainty of the respondent's belonging to the group $h = 2$ is low.

3. Chronic complainers are more likely to answer not preferring any appreciation → Lower evaluation levels of customer satisfaction in all groups are excessive. The uncertainty of the evaluation at a low rate in all groups is increased.

4. An average client does not support researches too much, generally, it is the exhibitionists who speak (answers are rather overestimating or underestimating) → The number of favourable evaluations in the group 1 and unfavourable in the group 3 is excessive. The uncertainty of the correctness of the level of the

respondent's evaluation in the group 1 is the higher, the higher the level of his evaluation is. The uncertainty of the level correctness of the respondent in the group 3 is the higher, the lower the level of his evaluation is.

These hypotheses represent the linguistically formulated mental models which will be formalized by computer through the fuzzy rule models in the following chapter.

To derive the fuzzification rate of the respondent's belonging to a group and the fuzzification of the evaluation of his satisfaction, the Mamdani fuzzy rule models which respect expert hypotheses were designed.

The FA_BSC system contains 3 language fuzzy models for individual groups of respondents ($h = 1, 2, 3$) – see Table 4.

The input linguistic variable THE RESPONDENT'S EVALUATION IN GROUPS *HODRh* has three linguistic values: Low (LOW), Middle (MDL) and High (HGH). They are formalized by three fuzzy sets – see Figure16.

The output linguistic variables THE RATE OF THE RESPONDENT'S BELONGING TO A GROUP *KNAL1* have four linguistic values: Low (LOW), Lowered (LWR), Increased (INC), and High (HGH), formalized by four fuzzy sets (Figure17).

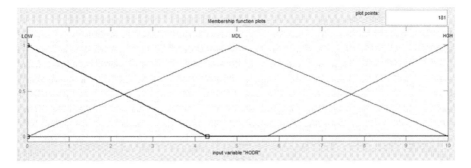

Figure 16. Membership Functions of Linguistic Values of the Input Variable *HODR*.

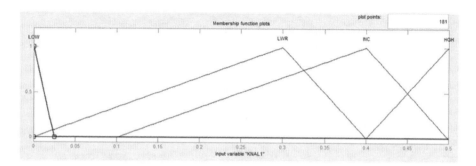

Figure 17. Membership Functions of Linguistic Values of the Output Variable *KNAL1*.

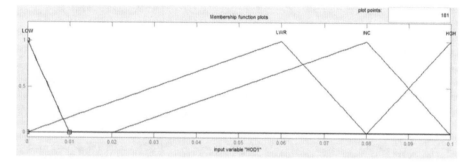

Figure 18. Membership Functions of Linguistic Values of the Output Variable *HOD1*.

The output linguistic variables THE RATE OF THE EVALUATION OF A RESPONDENT IN A GROUP *KHOD1* have four linguistic values: Low (LOW), Lowered (LWR), Increased (INC), and High (HGH), formalized by four fuzzy sets (Figure18).

The membership functions of the linguistic values of the output variables *KNAL2* and *KNAL3, KHOD2* and *KHOD3* are identical.

The rules of the fuzzy models (knowledge bases), deriving the output variables *KNALh*, respect the impacts of the hypotheses 1 and 2, the rules, deriving the output variables *KHODh*, respect the impacts of the hypotheses 3 and 4.

The FA_BSC system (Table 4) includes the rules for three fuzzy models *FA_BSC_H1, FA_BSC_H2,* and *FA_BSC_H3*, each of which is assigned for the estimation of the fuzzification rate of the level of the respondent's belonging to the group *KNALh* and the fuzzification rate of satisfaction evaluation *KHOD$_j$h* for individual respondents j = 1, 2, ..., K_h in the groups h = 1, 2, 3.

Table 4. Language fuzzy models of FA_BSC system

FA_BSC_H1
R1   IF (HODR1 is LOW) THEN (KNAL1 is LWR and KHOD1 is LWR)
R2   IF (HODR1 is MDL) THEN (KNAL1 is LOW and KHOD1 is LOW)
R3   IF (HODR1 is HGH) THEN (KNAL1 is HGH and KHOD1 is SNI)
FA_BSC_H2
R1   IF (HODR2 is LOW) THEN (KNAL2 is LWR and KHOD2 is INC)
R2   IF (HODR2 is MDL) THEN (KNAL2 is LOW and KHOD2 is LOW)
R3   IF (HODR2 is HGH) THEN (KNAL2 is LWR and KHOD2 is LOW)
FA_BSC_H3
R1   IF (HODR3 is LOW) THEN (KNAL3 is LWR and KHOD3 is HGH)
R2   IF (HODR3 is MDL) THEN (KNAL3 is LOW and KHOD3 is LOW)
R3   IF (HODR3 is HGH) THEN (KNAL3 is LOW and KHOD3 is LOW).

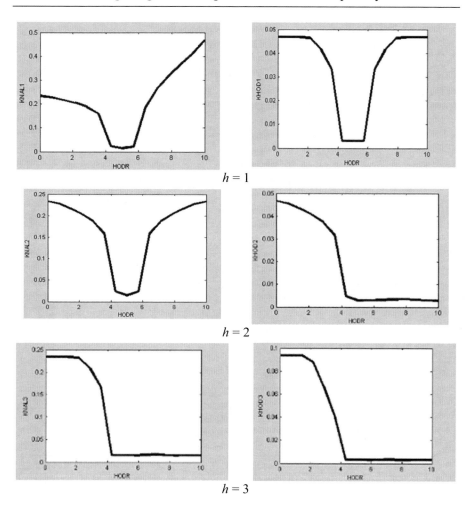

$h = 1$

$h = 2$

$h = 3$

Figure 19. Graphical Functional Dependencies of the Linguistic Variables.

The creation of a language model is easy, the compilation of a mathematical model requires experts. The expert can easily include any other rule which he himself followed in his mental model during the estimation of uncertainty into the structure of the language model. The fuzzy models FA_BSC_H1, FA_BSC_H2, and FA_BSC_H3 are implemented in the programming environment of the Fuzzy Toolbox package MATLAB.

Figure 19 shows graphical analytical courses of the dependencies of output variables *KNALh* and *KHODh* for individual groups of respondents, h = 1, 2, 3. The graphs were derived from the fuzzy models Table 1. Shapes in Figure 19 correspond with source hypotheses.

Table 5. Experimental data files

j	SURVEY A			SURVEY B		
	Aj,1	Aj,2	Aj,3	Aj,1	Aj,2	Aj,3
1	1	2	1	4	7	6
2	0	1	1	4	6	6
3	2	2	0	5	5	5
4	0	2	2	7	4	6
5	3	0	1	6	4	4
6	3	0	3	7	7	7
7	3	4	8	6	6	6
8	3	3	8	4	6	4
9	4	4	7	4	5	4
10	4	4	6	6	4	4
11	5	3	8	6	3	6
12	4	4	8	7	7	6
13	3	4	8	7	6	6
14	4	2	6	6	6	7
15	6	4	5	6	7	5
16	4	3	7	6	6	5
17	5	3	6	5	5	6
18	5	2	8	5	4	7
19	5	3	7	4	4	6
20	4	3	6	7	6	5
21	5	2	7	6	5	5
22	7	3	6	5	5	4
23	6	3	7	7	5	4
24	10	9	10	7	6	4
25	7	9	9	6	7	3
26	10	10	10	5	5	4
27	9	10	9	5	4	5
28	10	9	9	6	4	6
29	10	8	9	6	5	5
30	8	10	8	7	6	5

5.4. Verification of Fuzzy Models Functions

For the verification of fuzzy models functions, two data files with the evaluation of 30 respondents in 3 groups h = 1, 2, 3 were deliberately generated – Table 5. The Survey A file includes sub-files with higher levels of evaluation in the marginal areas of the scale (grey cells), leading, according to the expressed hypotheses, to the indices of satisfaction with a higher uncertainty. The Survey B file is formed by sub-files without a higher level of evaluation in the marginal areas of the scale, leading to the satisfaction indices with a lower uncertainty.

To calculate the BSC fuzzified criteria, the programming system for fuzzy arithmetic FA v1.00 was used [11]. The algorithms correspond to the Zadeh's extension principle and use the method of α-cuts.

In the following Figure 20, the graphical outputs of the calculation program FA are shown. The shapes of the membership functions of the fuzzy global evaluation IS (labeled as *ISx*) are stated, both for the data from the *DATA 1* file (the upper one), and for the data from the *DATA 2* file (the lower one).

The legend is on the right side of the figures. The level of uncertainty of a particular fuzzy number is represented by the width of the carrier of its membership functions ΔIS. According to the characteristics of data files, the global uncertainty of index *IS* calculated from the first file DATA1 (ΔS_{GLOB}= 1,532) is greater than the one calculated from the file DATA2 (ΔS_{GLOB}= 1,063).

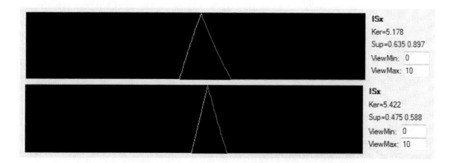

Figure 20. Membership Function of the Fuzzy Numbers of Global Evaluation.

CONCLUSION

In the case of the CSR study, a model of a hierarchical expert system which evaluates the influence of economic entities on the social environment was presented. The core of the system – corporate social responsibility – was described in detail. Four main areas – pillars of the corporate social responsibility were stated. These have an indisputable influence on the environment and the level of life of the society.

The proposed model, as it was simulated, deduces correct results and thus provides the possibility to process non-quantifiable facts and phenomena. It examines the behaviour of economic entities from four basic perspectives. However, these areas are not the only ones and their number is not final. The proposed model is of a developmental nature, the input variables and rules can be expanded and varied, again based on expert knowledge, the verbal description of these variables and their language evaluation by weights, measures or degrees of fulfilment of a particular criterion.

The probability model will make it possible to recognize and predict the behaviour, efficiency or the degree of involvement of particular economic entities in defined areas and it can also evaluate this involvement by verbal degrees. On the basis of such a finding, it is possible to predict the behaviour of the whole economy to a certain extent and perceive and include the so far unattainable and incalculable values into the macroeconomic development. Macroeconomic predictions based on the results found could be much more credible than those based on the hard indicators only.

The proposed probability model focuses on corporate social responsibility, however, it is open and can be modified easily. In the described areas of CSR, we can further expand the number and depth of the input variables and evaluate each of them by subjective probability degrees. In such a way, the proposed model can be refined, e.g., by depicting the specifics of the particular types of economic entities as well as incorporating the newly emerging activities in CSR.

The main goal of the case study Supplier Suitability is to analyse the decision-making task of the choice of the supplier, leading to a definition of its partial subtasks and a suggestion of a corresponding language model expert system. The partial goals of the paper are the presentation of the current trends in the area of the expert system use for the supplier choice, presentation of the principles and processes of synthesis of the fuzzy oriented expert systems for the solution of fragmentary subtasks, integration of a global hierarchic expert system, simulation confirmation of the system function on the example of the task of choice from two current and two new suppliers and, finally, the analysis and outlook onto the direction of further research.

The structure of the suggested and presented decision-making expert system reflects the original approach of the authors. Eight fragmentary expert modules, solving fragmentary decision-making tasks, are integrated into the hierarchic structure of the global expert system. An open structure which can be complemented with new rules (new knowledge) at any time is an important feature of the language models.

The function of the expert systems was verified by simulation experiments. These experiments are focused on the examination of two current and two new suppliers. The accuracy of function was then analysed and commented on. The difference between the estimation of the expert and the system is on a level corresponding to the technology of the solution used.

The advantage of this solution is the simplicity and transparency of its application with the possibility of the combination of various viewpoints on the potential suppliers. The main limitation is the current evaluation of new suppliers with limited input data (estimation by average).

On the basis of the undertaken analysis, it can be said that the new method is operable. The direction for further research can be the addition of further, e.g., environmental criteria to the new supplier evaluation model.

The case study BSC presents the methodology of creating linguistic fuzzy models for uncertainty measures determination within the Balanced Scorecard framework, built on the basis of subjective expert hypotheses. It shows the formalization of hypotheses based on the IF- THEN fuzzy models and respondents' answers in the form of fuzzy numbers. Numerical calculations show accuracy and efficiency of the proposed analytical algorithms, fuzzy algorithms, and fuzzy models. The uncertainty measure informs the managers about their vagueness.

Using fuzzy arithmetic and fuzzy logic allows us to handle and process vagueness which is often included in multidimensional performance measurement systems. The difference between the fuzzy type of uncertainty and stochastic uncertainty is that fuzzy does not require the knowledge (or estimation) of distribution functions, mean values, standard errors, etc. Fuzzy arithmetic is able to operate without this information therefore it can be used in areas with lack of knowledge of these parameters.

Moreover – fuzzy logic is also able to handle linguistic models such as "Certain group of customers is more pessimistic than the other." This suggests that it is possible to compute and process experts´ opinions with all the advantages (for example computers can easily process continuously) in software environment.

Even though the fuzzy background of the model and its processing requires a highly skilled professional in the field of fuzzy arithmetic and fuzzy logic, according to the actual knowledge of managers and management accountants who deal with the BSC, the design of the model is very easy and simple. So are the adjustments of the developed model for the latest or new knowledge and expertise. The easiness results from the fact that the fuzzy model is based on the mental model of a stakeholder – in this case managers and accountants who are interested in the performance of a business entity in the area of a customer perspective within the Balanced Scorecard. The model is designed using the same terms and verbal statements as normally expressed and used inside the companies. Therefore, the first important result of using fuzzy logic is that the uncertainty of such type can be handled and processed.

The second important result is the fuzzy uncertainty itself and its width. This information can be discussed in two ways. How reliable / non-fuzzy our information is (information which is more fuzzy can be treated as less useful than the less fuzzy one). Reliability is a crucial attribute of the accounting information. It is so significant that it is explicitly mentioned in the conceptual framework of the IAS / IFR. This chapter shows how to use the fuzzy logic and fuzzy arithmetic to handle the issue of reliability. The second way how this can be used is the message which a company gives to its customers – the fuzzier the response from the customers is, the less clear and understandable message the customers perceive.

From the managerial perspective these models show how to process and numerically express the vagueness of the multidimensional performance measurement systems or frameworks, such as the Balanced Scorecard is. This vagueness is immanent for all non-financial perspectives included in the BSC framework (and from the financial perspective, vagueness is highly probable especially in estimations, deferred accounts, etc.). The fuzzy type of uncertainty is therefore an important attribute of managerial information and is relevant for decision-making. Even though that management accounting puts less importance on the reliability (which can be expressed as vagueness) and more on the relevance and timeliness, still the information about fuzziness serves as another important attribute of managerial information. Fuzzy vagueness represents a relevant attribute of information, especially if the information is related to or derived from human mental models.

The vagueness is not only a relevant attribute of information but it is also important information itself. The intensity of vagueness, its development through the time – in this chapter related to the customer perspective of the BSC framework – is a relevant and important message for decision makers, as it shows not only the quality of information but also represents how clear and understandable message customers receive from the company. Vagueness related to the customer perspective of the BSC therefore can represent a measure of how well / bad the company communicates with customers, whether it is readable for its customers, whether the perception of the company by the customers is aligned with the intended picture.

The chapter introduces the expert systems used for simulation of the decision-making activity of experts when dealing with complex tasks in the field of economy. The introduced expert systems are able to effectively use uncertainties which take their source from inaccurate, incomplete, inconsistent input data, vague concepts of linguistic formulations of the rules, and uncertain knowledge.

The inclusion of uncertainty in the methods of calculations of economic indicators and criteria opens a new dimension of the assessment and application of their values.

REFERENCES

[1] Russel, S., & Norvig, P. (2010). *Artificial Intelligence – A Modern Approach* (3). New Yersey, US: Pearson Education.

[2] Kelemen, J., & Romportl, J., & Zackova, J., & Beyond, E. (2012). *Artificial Intelligence: Contemplations, Expectations, Applications.* Heidelberg, Germany: Springer.

[3] Dvořák, J. (2004). *Expert Systems.* Brno, CR: Technical University Brno, Brno, (in Czech).

[4] Mařík, V. & Štěpánková, O., & Lažanský, J. (1997). *Artificial Intelligence 2.* Praha, CR: ACADEMIA.

[5] *FEL EX Expert 1.0 – User Manual.* (2012). Praha, CR: CERTICON (in Czech).

[6] Buckley, J. J., & Siler, W. (2005). *Fuzzy Expert Systems and Fuzzy Reasoning. Theory and Applications.* NY, United States: John Wiley & Sons Inc.

[7] Mohan, C., (2010). *Fuzzy Set Theory and Fuzzy Logic.* United Kingdom: Anshan Ltd.

[8] Novák, V., & Perfilieva, I., & Močkoř, J. (1999). *Mathematical Principles of Fuzzy Logic.* Boston , USA: Kluwer.

[9] Mordeson, J. N. & Nair, P. S. (2001). *Fuzzy Mathematics.* Heidelberg, Germany: Physica-Verlag.

[10] Hanss, M. (2005). *Applied Fuzzy Arithmetic: An Introduction with Engineering Applications*. Germany: Springer-Verlag Berlin And Heidelberg Gmbh & Co. Kg.

[11] Keprt, A. (2012). Fuzzy arithmetics programme system using α-cuts. *Economy-Management-Inovation, 3*, 38-49, (in Czech).

[12] Crane, A. (2008). *The Oxford handbook of corporate social responsibility*. New York, USA: Oxford University Press.

[13] Geva, Aviva. (2008). Three Models of Corporate Social Responsibility: Interrelationships between Theory, Research, and Practice [online]. www:http://doi.wiley.com/10.1111/j.1467-8594. 2008.00311.x.

[14] Green Paper. (2001). Promoting a European Framework for Corporate Social Responsibility, [online]. www:http://bit.ly/ 1TGkk52.

[15] ISO 26 000. (2010). *Guidance on social responsibility*. [online]. https://www.iso.org/obp/ui/#iso:std:iso:26000:ed-1:v1:en.

[16] *MATLAB - The MathWorks-MATLAB and Simulink for Technical Computing*. http://www.mahworks.com.

[17] Eshtehardian, E., & Ghodousi, P. & Bejanpour, A. (2013). Using ANP and for the Supplier Selection in the Construction and Civil Engineering Companies; Case Study of Iranian Company. *KSCE Journal of Civil Engineering, 17(2),* 262-270.

[18] Osiro, L., & Lima-junior, F. R., & Carpinetti. L. C. R. (2014). A fuzzy logic approach to supplier evaluation for development. *International Journal of Production Economics, 153,* 95–112.

[19] Awasthi, A., & Chauhan, S., & Goyal, S. K. (2010). A fuzzy multicriteria approach for evaluating environmental performance of suppliers. *International Journal of Production Economics, 126 (2),* 370-378.

[20] Kumar, D., & Pal Singh, O. (2013). A fuzzy logic based decision support system for evaluation of suppliers in supply chain management practices. *Mathematical and Computer Modelling, 58,* 1679–1695.

[21] Aksoy, A., & Ozturk, N. (2011). Supplier selection and performance evaluation in just-in-time production environments. *Expert Systems with Applications*, *38,* 6351–6359.

[22] Shu, M. H., & Wu, H. C. (2009). Quality-based supplier selection and evaluation using fuzzy data. *Computers and Industrial Engineering*, *57 (3),* 1072-1079.

[23] Razmi, J., & Rafiei, H., & Hshemi, M. (2009). Designing a decision support system to evaluate and select suppliers using fuzzy analytic network process. *Computers and Industrial Engineering, 57 (4),* 1282-1290.

[24] Kaplan, R. S., & Norton, D. P. (1996). Using the Balanced Scorecard as a Strategic Management System. *Harvard Business Review 74, No. 1,* 75–85.

[25] Bobillo, F., & Delgado, M., & Gómez-Romero, J., & López, E. (2009). A semantic fuzzy expert system for a fuzzy balanced scorecard. *Expert Systems with Applications 36, No. 1,* 423-433.

[26] Möller, B., & Beer, M. (2004). *Fuzzy Randomness – Uncertainty in Civil Engineering and Computational Mechanics*. Berlin, Germany: Springer.

In: Expert Systems
Editor: Darrel Ryan

ISBN: 978-1-53612-503-0
© 2017 Nova Science Publishers, Inc.

Chapter 2

A RULE-BASED EXPERT SYSTEM FOR HETEROGENEOUS DATA SOURCE INTEGRATION IN SMART GRID SYSTEMS

J. I. Guerrero*, PhD, Antonio García,
Enrique Personal, PhD, Antonio Parejo,
Francisco Pérez, PhD, and Carlos León, PhD
Department of Electronic Technology
University of Seville, Seville, Spain

ABSTRACT

The arrival of new technologies related to Smart Grids and the resulting ecosystem of applications and management systems pose challenges or problems to be solved. In this way, the compatibility with databases of the traditional and the new management systems, related to initiatives of new technologies, have given rise to different formats and architectures. Due to this, a heterogeneous data source integration system is essential to update these systems for the new Smart Grid reality. In this sense, there are several problems which need to be solved: information

---

* Corresponding Author Email: juaguealo@us.es.

integration, incomplete data model definition, understanding of database models, evolution of technologies and modelling information.

Additionally, it is necessary to take advantage of the information that Smart Grids provide. The Smart Grids must provide new services to the consumers and operators, integrating the information from all the partners, ensuring the information protection and security.

At first, this chapter briefly treats an analysis of the proposed problems and makes a bibliographical review. Following this review, it proposes a solution for heterogeneous data source integration in the information standard formats, based on Rule Based Expert System (RBES) to implement a metadata mining process. Later, it describes the process of automatic modelling in which the proposed RBES support in the data mining technique applications, based on the results of metadata mining process. Finally, it describes the application issues of the proposed solution in real cases.

Keywords: expert systems, metadata mining, smart grid, data integration, big data

INTRODUCTION

The Smart Grids have provided a great scope of solutions to manage and control the power grid. Additionally, the Smart Cities propose a wider vision of Smart Grids, extending this model to other utilities and services which could have a city: health, claims, transport, communication, etc. These new scenarios pose new advantages for the current society, increasing the quantity of information, the services, etc. The analysis of information and services is a very complex task. Traditionally, the analysis of information in all these cases could provide some patterns or relationships between parameters. Thus, the data mining and computational intelligence techniques are broadly applied to solve these problems. The utilization of these techniques can provide patterns or relationships between parameters, which would manually be very difficult to get.

Currently, the new technologies related to Smart Grids have increased the quantity of available information. This new information is provided by a wide variety of systems, which are mainly implemented by Intelligent

Information Systems (IISs). Thus, the intelligent analytical tools are essential to implement this type of system, coordinated with robust and secure infrastructures. However, the increasing of available information makes the manual analysis of information impossible, so the information should be analyzed using automatic and advanced techniques for data analysis. Additionally, the new technologies related to information management could improve the analysis techniques. The new architectures based on Hadoop, Spark, or other frameworks of information management are essential to implement the new scenario provided by Smart Grids. Moreover, the technologies related to High Performance Computing (HPC) increase the capability of systems analyzing, making it quicker and attaining a higher quantity of information.

However, the new ecosystem implemented in Smart Grids needs some special capabilities. These systems should be able to work with information of a traditional system, and also use this information to enrich the model with new information, so the deployment of these systems cannot be performed quickly. The update of all the facilities of the distribution grid take a lot of time, economic, and technical costs. Thus, in the starting stages of updating a power grid, traditional and modern power grids must coexist in the same grid.

PROBLEM DESCRIPTION

The traditional systems in the power distribution grids usually have databases with different data structure. The new technologies related to Smart Grids have provided the advantage of new and advanced functions. Although these new systems are based on the usage of sensor networks and information systems, the systems need the information from the older ones, integrating information from the heterogeneous data sources. In this sense, there are several problems which need to be solved: information integration, incomplete data model definition, understanding of database models, evolution of technologies, and modelling information.

Information Integration

The new systems need to take advantage of an old and new data sources. Thus, the integration of these heterogeneous data sources is very difficult, because each database has their own structure. This data source should be translated into a common format. In this way, the information standards provide a good source for a Common Information Models (CIM). Organizations, like International Electrotechnical Committee (IEC) and Distributed Management Task Force (DMTF), have provided each CIM standard. The IEC CIM is used in utility companies, mainly in power sector, and DMTF CIM is a generic model, mainly focused on the system management. Both standards are complex and demand a high level of knowledge in order to be applied on database system. Therefore, the automatic information integration could provide a supporting system in the implementation of new systems based on data from the old systems.

Additionally, the information integration could be necessary for the application of the analytic tools. In this case, the integration should be made of data warehouse structure. Thus, the system needs to generate new structures from old databases focused on one or more topics. The application of this type of integration could be also used for reporting, visualization, etc.

Incomplete Data Model Definition

The data structures and the models of relational databases are not often completely implemented. Frequently, there are several things that are lacking in the database structure: foreign keys, primary keys, constraints of specific columns, etc. The lack of any of these components make more difficult to understand stored information; although these lacks make the implementation of interfaces easier, being the joining of tables performed in queries.

There are several problems related to the incomplete data model definition. For example, in the case of lack of foreign keys, the cardinality of the non-specified relationships could be definitive for classification of the content, and, consequently, the adaptation of this information to the new integrated model. Moreover, other type of relationships like self-relationships, could make very difficult the interpretation of the information model.

Understanding of Database Models

Each system involved in power distribution grids usually has a different structure: charging management for electrical vehicles (Richardson, Flynn, & Keane, 2012; Sousa, Morais, Vale, Faria, & Soares, 2012), energy management systems for buildings (La, Chan, & Soong, 2016; Wang, Wang, & Yang, 2012), and distribution systems (Zidan & El-Saadany, 2012). The use of information standards simplifies the understanding information stage, in any process of system, data mart or modelling development. The information standards provide a CIM to store all information about the power grid and management systems, for example: IEC with 61970, 61968 and 62325 standards, and DMTF with CIM, RedFish, etc. Although, the systems developed for new paradigm of Smart Grid are usually based on them, the old systems are usually based on third party or proprietary information models. Thus, the integration of these types of data sources usually requires one or more experts with advanced knowledge about the specific information model.

Evolution of Technologies

The evolution of power grids from a traditional model to the named Smart Grid has been provoked by several factors: the generalized liberalization of electric sector, the pressuring to adopt an environmentally sustainable system, and the technological development of Information and Communication Technology (ICT) scope.

This evolution has provided the deployment of a set of systems previously unavailable: from the massive deployment of Distributed Energy Resources (DER), including the electric vehicle; the massive deployment of Advanced Metering Infrastructure (AMI) highlighting the Smart Meters (SM), which generate an exponential growth in the volume of available data, requiring the development and application of new tools of information treatment in grid management topic (Analytics). They are the seed of new developments in new applications in this scope:

- Meter Data Management (MDM).
- Demand Response (DR).
- Distributed Energy Resources Management Systems (DERMS).
- Virtual Power Plants (VPPs) and microgrid.
- Electric Vehicles, infrastructure management.

These applications require the abilities of monitorization, modelling, simulation, analysis, and forecasting. These abilities start from heterogeneous data sources: weather, traffic, consumption measures (at level of Distributed System Operator (DSO), or client), asset information, geographical, power market data, etc.

Currently, the development of new technologies is faster than the market's ability to apply them, being more evident in the electrical distribution field. Particularly, the technologies related to the information management developed for power distribution companies needs to evolve the systems to take advantage from the new functionalities.

Modelling Information

The new technologies based on Smart Grid systems increase the volume of databases. These databases need powerful algorithms to model the information. Additionally, the information from older system provides several references in order to evaluate the impact of these new technologies, i.e., by means of Key Performance Indicators (KPI), or to get better models.

Two popular methodologies are used in data mining: SEMMA (Sample, Explore, Modify, Model, and Assess) and CRISP-DM (Cross-Industry Standard Process for Data Mining). These two methodologies are notably different, but both methodologies have steps for data understanding and preparation. For example, in SEMMA: Sample, Explore and Modify, and in CRISP-DM: Business Understanding, Data Understanding, and Data Preparation. These steps take a long time, and to carry them out, companies usually need staff with both highly specialized background knowledge of data mining and familiarity with the domain of the problem to be solved.

Additionally, in certain cases, an integration of heterogeneous data collections should be performed to provide a sample for a data mining application or a data source for a different framework, for example, security appliances (Ruj & Nayak, 2013). In the area of power systems, Smart Grids pose new scenarios with great quantities of information that require big data infrastructures and real time processing. These infrastructures should integrate the new data generated and the old data provided by the traditional systems (e.g., SCADAs). The Smart Grid ecosystem compounds a great quantity of systems, such as charging management for electrical vehicles (Richardson et al., 2012; Sousa et al., 2012), energy management systems for buildings (La et al., 2016; Wang et al., 2012), and distribution systems (Zidan & El-Saadany, 2012).

BIBLIOGRAPHICAL REVIEW

The main research related to metadata mining applies to documents (Campos & Silva, 2000) and multimedia contents (Wong, 1999), and they are focused on knowledge discovery (Yi, Sundaresan, & Huang, 2000) or content classification (Yi & Sundaresan, 2000). Other references are focused on the usage of metadata over several types of contents: (Şah & Wade, 2012) proposed a novel automatic metadata extraction framework, which is based on a novel fuzzy method for automatic cognitive metadata generation and uses different document parsing algorithms to extract rich metadata from multilingual enterprise content. (Asonitis, Boundas, Bokos, & Poulos, 2009) proposed an automated tool for characterizing new video files, using metadata schemas.

Some other references deal with heterogeneous data integration. (Alemu & Stevens, 2015) proposed an efficient metadata filtering in order the users apply metadata and thus enhance the findability and discoverability of the information objects. (Fermoso et al., 2009) proposed a new software tool called XDS (eXtensible Data Sources) that integrates data from relational databases, native eXtensible Markup Language (XML) databases, and XML documents. This framework integrates all information from heterogeneous databases to a XML-based format, such as MODS (Metadata Object Description Schema).

There are some references which pose the heterogeneous data integration providing models based on the analysis of available information. (Liu, Liu, Wu, & Ma, 2013) propose a Heterogeneous Data Integration Model (HDIM) based on the comparison and analysis of the current existing data integration approaches. On this HDIM, a pattern-mapping-based system called UDMP is designed and implemented. This approach tries to improve the rapid development of the Internet of Things (IoT). Moreover, (Lu & Song, 2010) proposed a heterogeneous data integration for Smart Grids. The authors described a model based on XML and ontology combined with cloud services to solve the heterogeneous problem from the syntax and semantics. They also tested with Supervisory Control and Data Acquisition (SCADA) data to validate the model. Some of these models were provided by means of an algebra. This tool is especially interesting because the mathematical description was more accurate and efficient. (Tang, Zhang, & Xiao, 2005) propose a capability object conceptual model to capture a rich variety of query-processing capabilities of sources and outline an algebra to compute the set of mediator-supported queries based on the capability limitations of the sources they integrate. This algebra is used in several works.

Additionally, there are a lot of studies and researches related to heterogeneous data integration based on, for instance, XML (Fengguang, Xie, & Liqun, 2009) (Su, Fan, & Li, 2010) (Lin, 2009), Lucene and XQuery (Tianyuan, Meina, & Xiaoqi, 2010), and OGSA-DAI (Gao & Xiao, 2013). In the same way, heterogeneous data integration has been applied on many areas, such as Livestock Products Traceability (X. d Chen & Liu, 2009), safety production (Han, Tian, & Wu, 2009), management information systems (Hailing & Yujie, 2012), medical information (Shi, Liu, Xu, & Ji, 2010), and web environments (Fan & Gui, 2007).

There are also examples of the application of data mining mixed with heterogeneous data source integration. These types of solutions increase the capability of solution to adapt it to different and heterogeneous data sources. (Cao, Chen, & Jiang, 2007) proposed a framework of a self-Adaptive Heterogeneous Data Integration System (AHDIS), based on ontology, semantic similarity, web service and XML techniques, which can be regulated dynamically. (Merrett, 2001) use On-Line Analytical Processing (OLAP) and data mining to illustrate the advantages for the relational algebra of adding the metadata type attribute and the transpose operator.

Currently, one of the main objectives of integrating the information is to analyse it. The proposed solution integrates heterogeneous data sources in specific and standard structures, and automatically applies data mining techniques. Thus, for example, some references related to this topic apply specific algorithms. (Li, Kang, & Gao, 2007) proposed a high-level knowledge modelled by Ordinary Differential Equations (ODEs) discovered automatically in dynamic data by an Asynchronous Parallel Evolutionary Modelling Algorithm (APHEMA). The data mining techniques are mainly used for forecast parameters. (J. Chen, Li, Lau, Cao, & Wang, 2010) proposed detecting automated load curve data cleansing based on the B-Spline smoothing and Kernel smoothing to automatically cleanse corrupted and missing data. (Hoiles & Krishnamurthy, 2015) proposed a nonparametric demand forecasting based on Least Squares Support Vector Machine (LS-SVM). The main lack of these references is that they did not automatically select the parameters to model, but they are selected previously. In the proposed solution, the parameters to model are automatically selected in metadata mining stage.

GENERAL DESCRIPTION

The functional architecture of the proposed solution is shown in Figure 1. This solution is based on the use of different information analysis: metadata mining, text mining, data mining, and rule based expert system. Each of these techniques provides the ability to treat different types of data, even the metadata. The merging of these technologies allow to solve the problem of heterogeneous data source integration. Although several techniques related to the machine learning are used in this solution, it is mainly based on the knowledge, so the core of the proposed solution is the RBES. Thus, the proposed solution is limited to a knowledge domain related to Smart Grids and utilities. Although it has this limitation, it has a very big scope of the applications for present and future initiatives related to Smart Grid and utilities. In this sense, the deployment of Smart Grid ecosystem or a specific system in a Smart Grid is quicker because the proposed solution designs a specific Extract, Transform, and Load (ETL) for the new systems based on the information standards. Moreover, the integration of information can be optionally stored in data warehouses (with star or snowflake structure) to use the information in analysis processes. Additionally, the integration process can be applied in any distributed system with a high security level, due to the system only uses metadata. Finally, the proposed system includes a data and text mining engine to provide basic models for each parameter identified in the data sources, using different data and text mining techniques.

The information flow (specified by the arrows) and functional architecture is shown in Figure 1. The metadata from data sources is gathered by the Metadata Mining Engine using the query engine. The Metadata Mining Engine generates different information as parameters. Some of these parameters include the application of different techniques related to text mining, fuzzy logic, and Natural Language Processing

(NLP). The metadata are characterized and classified in different aggregation levels. The classification process is supported by the proposed Rule Based Expert System (RBES). Thus, in some stages, the RBES works as a Decision Support System (DSS). The RBES has several rules that are based on the indicators generated in the metadata mining process and the results of queries. When the system has classified all metadata from all data sources, the Dynamic ETL Engine performs the integration. There are two possibilities: according to an information standard or data warehouse (star or snowflake structure). If the user requires it, the integrated information can be modelled by the Data and Text Mining Engine. This engine performs an analysis according to the metadata mining information, to obtain the best model for each selected parameter. This process is supported by the RBES, too.

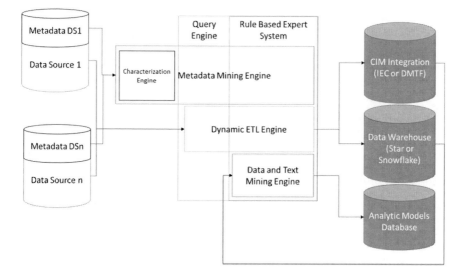

Figure 1. Flow and architecture overview.

METADATA MINING

The relational databases are one of the most widespread type of databases applied in past and present systems, even in future solution based on Smart Grids. The metadata mining process is based on the metadata extracted from relational databases. The study of other type of databases is in research stage, but the relational databases are the beginning point. The metadata mining methodology is the same in all these cases. The flow diagram is shown in Figure 2. In the case of relational databases, this methodology has several steps:

1. Relational database identification. The proposed system has been tested with relational databases: MySQL, IBM DB2, Oracle Database, PostgreSQL, Microsoft SQL Server, and HBase. The identification of the relational database management system provides:
   a. Query language.
   b. Specific considerations about the RDBMS (Relational Data Base Management System).
   c. The name and structure of system tables.
   This process was simultaneously applied to several data sources.
2. Metadata extraction from system tables of database. The MDBS identification provides the definition of SQL (Statement Query Language) sentences to extract the metadata and, in some cases, the different aspects of SQL. This process is supported by the RBES.
3. Execution of grouping queries. After the metadata extraction, a process of the identification from the different entities is performed. For each entity, the system generates a sequence of SQL queries to extract aggregated data from each column separately. In this way, the information anonymization is warranted, because it is not possible to cross information from different columns.
4. Characterization Process. The characterization of different entities is performed over tables, columns, relationships, etc.

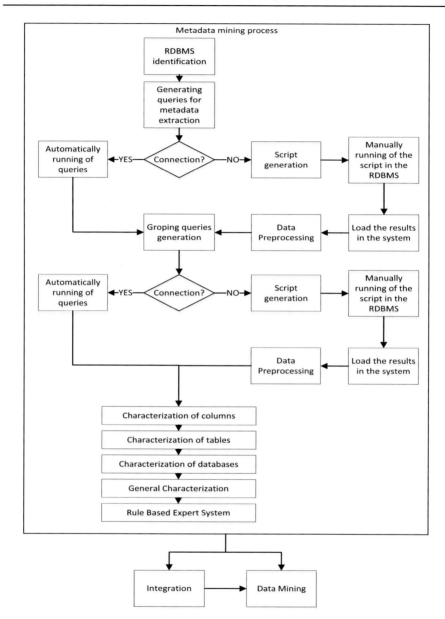

Figure 2. Metadata mining process flow chart.

5. Integration of information. The integration of information according to the results of characterization is performed, according to the information standards or data warehouse. This process is supported by RBES.

   Query design or data extraction. There are two options:

   a. Performing the integration. The queries are created and designed as an ETL, supporting by the RBES. Then, the integration is made of running the queries.

   b. Creating only the queries. The queries are created and designed, the system runs the queries when the users or other subsystems need it.

7. Data mining. After the creation of the database or scheme, the system applies a pool of data mining and text mining technique to obtain models from information. This process is supported by the RBES and the results of Metadata Mining process.

8. Results. All results are included as part of the final database scheme.

METADATA EXTRACTION FROM SYSTEM TABLES OF DATA SOURCES

Several queries to extract system tables are performed according to the database identified. These queries are automatically generated according to the identified RDBMS. The system provides two options to perform the queries:

- In a system whose RDBMS is not directly accessible, the system provides a SQL script. The user has to run this script in the command line of the RDBMS. The results of the script usually are several text files (one per system table) and these text files are loaded in the system. This information is pre-processed in order to correct mistakes and format errors.

- The system runs the queries through a connection with RDBMS. The pre-processing step is easier than in the other case because the direct connection reduces the mistakes and errors in the interpretation of extracted information.

EXECUTION OF GROUPING QUERIES

The grouping queries are executed for each column of each table to obtain information regarding: the different values of the column, the frequency of each value, the absolute and relative frequencies of each value, and different statistical information about the distribution of values.

This information is mixed with the information from the previous step if there is a statistical information regarding the column in the system tables. Occasionally, the statistical information in the system tables is empty because the database was not analysed by RDBMS tools.

The results of grouping queries are stored in different tables. For example, the grouping query for columnA in Table 1 in standard SQL (Statement Query Language) was:

SELECT tableA. columnA, COUNT(*) AS counter_tableA_columnA
FROM tableA
GROUP BY tableA. columnA
ORDER BY tableA. columnA;

This query provides a table with two columns: columnA and counter. The first column contains all the possible values of the column. The second column contains the number of the register which has the corresponding value. This table is stored in the target database. The name of the table will be a combination of the table and column names: table1_column.

CHARACTERIZATION ENGINE

The metadata mining process is executed in several characterization stages: columns, tables, data source, and general. The general characterization is simultaneously performed with the columns, tables, and data source characterization. This means that if we have three data sources four characterizations are simultaneously performed.

Characterization of Columns

The characterization of a column depends on the data type. The first step is to classify the column in one of these categories: Numerical, Text, Timestamp, Object, Binary, or Other column. Each category is characterized according to different indexes and coefficients with statistical information about the contents of columns. They have some indexes and coefficients in common, which are related to the frequency of null, blank, and default values.

Additionally, the relationships between different columns to the other columns are calculated with two indexes:

- Fuzzy relationship coefficient with each column. This is an array of indexes, one per column in the database. Each element of this array establishes the relationship between different fields according to the name of the column. The index calculation is based in the application of a fuzzy algorithm to match the column name with other column names. The index can have a value between 0 and 1; zero indicates that there isn't any relationship, and one indicates that the columns are related.
- Relationship coefficient with each column. This is an array of indexes, one per column in the database. Each element of this array establishes the relationship between different columns according to

the registered values. First, the algorithm compares the data type, after that, the values.

These indexes and the information of the number of registers provide information about cardinality of relationships.

The profile of numerical columns contains information about data type, length, precision, column description, and constraints. Some statistical information is calculated: maximum, minimum, standard deviation, average, median, mode, and variation coefficient.

The profile of text columns contains information about data type, length, char set, column description, and constraints. Some statistical information is calculated: maximum length, minimum length, average length, standard deviation length, maximum number of words, minimum number of words, and average word length. Additionally, a dictionary is generated using text mining techniques. This dictionary is used to calculate the relationship coefficient with each column. The text mining technique attempts to elicit the text field concepts, structured or otherwise. A concept can comprise one or more words which represent an entity (e.g., action, and event). Natural Language Processing (NLP) methods are used to extract linguistic (e.g., words and phrases) and non-linguistic (e.g., dates and numbers) concepts. An interesting review of this technique and its use in information management systems is proposed in (Métais, 2002). The following set of functionalities are included:

a. Recognition of punctuation errors. These types of mistakes include the incorrect use of the accent, the period, the comma, the point and comma, the dividing bar, etc.

b. Recognition of spelling errors. A grouping fuzzy technology is applied. When concepts of the text are extracted, words with similar spelling (referring to the letters that compose it) or that are closely related are classified together. By applying this algorithm, mistakes of omission of letters, duplication of letters, or permutation of letters are corrected. This algorithm is used in the fuzzy relationship coefficient with each column calculation.

Although these mistakes are corrected before storing the concept in the dictionary, they are registered in the system in order to establish the level of wording of the column.

The profile of timestamp columns contains information about data type, format, column description, and constraints. Some statistical information is calculated: minimum, maximum, average time period between registers, minimum time period between registers, maximum time period between registers, values with the maximum number of registers, values with the minimum number of registers, average number of registers per value, standard deviation of number of registers per value, and values with the nearest number of registers to average number of registers per value. Additionally, a histogram of the number of registers per value is created. This histogram is normalized from 0 to 1, dividing the number of registers in each value by total number of registers. This information is used to calculate the relationship coefficient with each column.

The profile of object columns is used when the column contains information in a specific datatype defined in the RDBMSs. These data types are composed by different primitive types. If the system table contains information about this data type (sometimes this information is not accessible) the system associates several profiles to the column, one per primitive type, generating all the information previously described in each profile. Arrays are classified in this category.

The profile of binary column is used when the data type of a column stores binary information, for example images, documents, etc. Currently, the metadata mining only classifies the type of contents into the following categories: images, documents, video, technical, and other.

The profile of other columns is used when the column cannot be classified in the categories above. Normally, these columns are not used in the metadata mining process, and they are manually handled in order to establish a new profile. The encrypted columns are usually classified in this category.

Characterization of Tables

Each table on the selected data source is classified in one of the following categories: parametric information table, entity information table, personal information table, historical information table, complementary information table, bridge table, orphan table, and dummy table.

Additionally, some indicators are calculated for each table related to: relationships with other tables, self-relationships, coefficients and indicators of constraints, number of columns, number of each category of columns, and number of registers.

Characterization of Data Source

The characterization of the data source determines the coherence and reliability of the stored information, and it establishes the different indicators that will be used in automatic application of data mining techniques. These techniques try to establish models for prediction and classification of information. Additionally, the characterization includes information for automatic integration with other data sources.

- Database malleable indicator. This indicator establishes the potential for data analysis based on the information stored in the database. The number of columns with a high rate of useful information (columns with any possibility of application of any data mining technique) plus columns without useful information but with a high correlation coefficient with useful columns divided by the total number of columns.
- Database time analysis indicator. This indicator establishes the potential of temporal analysis. The calculation of this indicator is very similar to the "Database malleable indicator". This indicator

considers as useful columns, those columns with any possibility of application of any time analysis technique.

- Database classification analysis indicator. This indicator establishes the potential of application of classification and clustering techniques. The calculation of this indicator is very similar to the "Database malleable indicator". This indicator considers as useful columns those columns with any possibility of application of any classification or clustering technique.

- Database forecasting analysis indicator. This indicator establishes the potential of application of forecasting techniques. The calculation of this indicator is very similar to the "Database malleable indicator". This indicator considers as useful columns those columns with any possibility of application of any forecasting technique.

- Database text analysis indicator. This indicator establishes the potential of application of text mining techniques. The calculation of this indicator is very similar to the "Database malleable indicator". This indicator considers as useful columns, those columns with any possibility of application of any text mining technique.

- Cohesion indicator. This indicator shows the information cohesion. The orphan registers and tables are used to calculate this indicator. Additionally, if statistical information about the database is available, then this indicator is modified adding columns without queries.

- Replication indicator. This indicator shows the level of redundant information.

General Characterization

This characterization is simultaneously carried on with the characterization of each data source. The general characterization establishes the relationship between all the data sources characterized according to the method previously defined. In this characterization, all the previous steps are repeated, but considering all databases or data sources as the sole database. In this way, the characterization of tables, columns, relationships, and data sources are calculated again, but the name of the table includes the name of original data source ('data_sourceA.tableA' is tableA from data_sourceA). The new calculated indicators contain values according to all data sources. These new indicators have the prefix 'general'.

RBES AND INTEGRATION OF INFORMATION

The RBES has several rules that are based on the indicators generated in the metadata mining process and the results of queries. The proposed RBES implements a DSS. The RBES has 492 rules: 30 rules in Metadata Mining Engine, 352 rules in Dynamic ETL Engine, and 110 rules in Data and Text Mining Engine. Each of these rules has been obtained from experience in collaboration in around 20 research projects with utility companies. The common problem in these projects is the existence of different relational data sources (95% were relational databases), with different: data management systems, data model, scope, and, often, without defined foreign keys. The 30 rules in Metadata Mining Engine deal with technical metadata. The 352 rules in Dynamic ETL Engine deal with technical and informational metadata to create and run the ETL. These rules could be classified into:

- Dynamic rules. The antecedent and consequence of a dynamic rule are stored on a table. This really means that each dynamic rule is applied several times, depending on the coincidences between available information and the data stored in the dynamic rule antecedent. In this sense, several sets of rules could be identified by:
  - 95 rules deal with IEC Common Information Model (CIM).
  - 83 rules deal with DMTF CIM.

- − 32 rules deal with IEC CIM extensions.
- − 36 rules deal with DMTF CIM extensions.
- − 53 rules deal with constraints.
- − 33 rules deal with foreign constraints.
- • Static rules. These rules only have one antecedent and consequence. There are 20 rules which treat general topics to create and run the dynamic ETL.

The 110 rules in Data and Text Mining Engine could be classified in:

- • 96 dynamic rules, which deal with the selection and application of the most adequate method for each modelling process, according to technical and informational metadata and the characterization performed.
- • 14 static rules, which deal with the analysis of the results of modelling methods applied.

The integration of information from heterogeneous databases is accomplished by the application of general characterization in all classified databases. This module creates queries to integrate all information from columns and tables based on a decision support system based on the 352 rules. This DSS is part of a Dynamic ETL Engine and it is based on the information generated in the characterization of metadata mining process and on the results of several queries. The rules enable the queries to build the final query that integrates the information from different tables from different data sources. These queries are packed into ETL according to the target RDBMS. All tables with similar characterization are checked to be grouped according to the calculated cardinality. These new tables are characterized using the process previously described. The new values are compared with the original values in order to check the integration.

An example of these rules that involves several queries is shown below. This rule is used in the characterization of columns in order to calculate the cardinality of one side of the relationship. Some queries are performed to calculate it. This queries are:

- SELECT COUNT(tableA_columnA.columnA) AS count_tableA_columnA FROM tableA_columnA WHERE NOT(tableA.columnA IN (SELECT tableA.columnA FROM tableA_columnA, tableB_columnB WHERE tableA_columnA.columnA=tableB_columnB.columnB));
- SELECT MIN(counter_table.counterA) AS minA, MAX(counter_table.counterA) AS maxA, min(counter_table.counterB) AS minB, MAX(counter_table.counterB) AS maxB FROM (SELECT tableA_columnA.columnA, tableB_columnB.columnB, SUM(tableA_columnA.counter_tableA_columnA) AS counterA, SUM(tableB_columnB.counter_tableB_columnB) AS counterB FROM tableA_columnA, tableB_columnB where tableA_columnA.columnA=tableB_columnB.columnB group by tableA_columnA.columnA,tableB_columnB.columnB) AS counter_table;

The RBES uses the results of these queries and the calculated index to establish the cardinality of relation between columnA of table1 and columnB of Table2.

```
If fuzzy_relationship >=0.5 or
   relationship_coefficient >= 0.9 or
   exists defined constraint then
      If (minA==maxA and minA>1) or
         minA<maxA then
            (maximum cardinality is N)
      endif
      If (minA==maxA and minA==1) then
         (maximum cardinality is 1)
      endif
      If countA<>0 then
         (minimum cardinality is 0)
      else
         (minimum cardinality is 1)
      endif
endif
```

Currently, the process of checking the validity of the integration is performed by using several threshold parameters. These parameters are specified by the user or analyst. The automatic threshold parameter adjustment is in the research stage. Additionally, the user can filter orphan tables and bridge tables or avoid bridge tables.

GENERATION AND VALIDATION OF RULES

The rules generated for RBES were gathered from experience in several research projects related to utilities and Smart Grids. The most representative projects which take an important role in the creation of this solution have been previously published, but the main objective of these projects were not the heterogeneous data source integration, notwithstanding this capability was needed to get the results for each of these projects. Thus, the first prototype was not designed for all heterogeneous data sources, just only for the project, however, other projects showed the same problem. In this way, a general framework was created to integrate all information from different data sources in order to make easier the pre-processing stage of these projects. Some of these projects are described in:

- (Í. Monedero, Biscarri, León, Biscarri, & Millán, 2006), (León et al., 2011), (Juan I. Guerrero, León, Monedero, Biscarri, & Biscarri, 2014), and (Juan Ignacio Guerrero et al., 2016) describes The MIDAS Project. This project treats to reduce the non-technical losses applying data mining and computational intelligence to analyse the data from Endesa databases. Endesa databases have several data sources with different formats which need to be integrated in order to analyse it.
- (I. Monedero et al., 2015) describes a framework to detect water tampering in water utility, using data mining techniques. The data mining techniques are applied over data integrated from different data sources.

- (Personal, Guerrero, Garcia, Peña, & Leon, 2014) describes an application of Key Performance Indicators (KPI) Monitoring System to evaluate the integration of Smart Grid in front of traditional power grid. This system includes a Data Acquisition System. This system gathers information from different data sources in a unique data source in a format based on IEC CIM.
- (J.I. Guerrero, Personal, Parejo, García, & León, 2016) presents a framework to integrate systems in a Smart Grid ecosystem based on Web Service Mining and computational intelligence.

The first prototype of this framework only has a semi-automatic process to integrate tables, based on 239 configuration options, several of them derived from the number and nature of data sources. This tool was developed for MIDAS project and evolved and improved after several applications in MIDAS and other projects. After several applications of this prototype, several configuration rules were generated, validated, and the main structure of rules was designed. The proposed solution tries to integrate all information from all provided data sources in a specific standard format. When the framework could not integrate any part of any data source, the framework includes the necessary information to trace it. Thus, this information was manually analysed and new rules could be generated.

The proposed solution is the result of several iterations. The inference of new rules based on information from integration fails is still in research stage, but fuzzy logic and swarm intelligence methods have provided some interesting results.

INTEGRATION OF INFORMATION

The proposed system can integrate information in two different modes (the user can also configure the option of running both modes at the same time):

- According to the information of characterization. The system has been tested with several data sources. The intelligent ETL engine tries to create databases with star or extended-star architecture, in order to generate a data warehouse. This data warehouse is conditioned by the results of the characterization process, taking very high importance the indexes related to characterization of data source, and which shows where is the best information to create data mining and text mining modules. In this way, the data warehouse is optimized to support specific data mining or text mining models.

- According to the information of characterization and an information standard. Currently, the system only works with power distribution information standards. This system has been tested with information related to utilities, energy management, and information systems. The intelligent ETL engine can follow two standards: IEC CIM based on IEC 61970 and 61968 or DMTF CIM based on version 2.44.1 (but only applied to power grids). Currently, the utilization of other standards for health (HL7 and OpenEHR) are in the research stage.

The process is described in Figure 3. The integration of information includes several tables with information of characterization. This information was generated in metadata mining. The added tables are:

- GEN_CHAR. This table contains one register per data source, and contains information about the calculated indicators and data source description.
- DB_CHAR. This table contains one register per database, and contains information about the calculated indicators and database information. It is associated with data source described in GEN_CHAR.

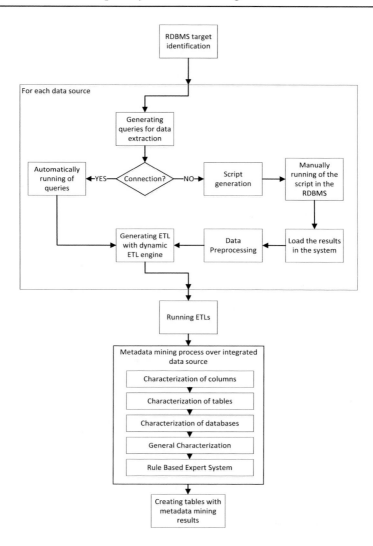

Figure 3. Integration flow chart.

- TAB_CHAR. This table contains one register per table, and contains information about the calculated indicators, relationship information, and table information. It is associated with data source (GEN_CHAR) and database (DB_CHAR).
- COL_CHAR. This table contains one register per column, and contains information about the calculated indicators, relationship information, and table information. It is associated with data

source   (GEN_CHAR),   database   (DB_CHAR),   datatype (DT_CHAR), and table (TAB_CHAR)

- CONS_CHAR. This table contains one register per constraint, and contains information about constraints and the associated table and column. It is associated with column (COL_CHAR) and table (TAB_CHAR).
- DT_CHAR. This table contains one register per component of data type, and contains information about data types.

Additionally, the information from the integrated resource is described by similar tables with 'I' prefix: I_DB_CHAR, I_TAB_CHAR, I_COL_ CHAR, I_CONS_CHAR, and I_DT_CHAR.

These tables have several additional columns to store information that will be generated in the data mining stage.

DATA EXTRACTION

The data extraction stage depends on whether there is a direct connection to the data source. When the data source is protected, and it is not possible to have a direct connection or remote connection, the queries are executed by a script generated by the system, and the user runs the script in an authorized client. The script provides several text files with information from each table. The user loads these files into the system.

However, when the system has a direct or remote connection with the data source, the extraction is automatically performed with authorization from the user.

DATA MINING

The data mining module is guided by information generated in the characterization stage, supported by an intelligent system based on 110 rules. In the first place, a feature selection is performed to associate a support index to each column. This feature selection is performed for each column as a target. In this way, each column has one value associated with it.

Currently, a threshold is manually specified to use the different columns. The value assigned for each method is established based on experience, although the user could modify that value if it is necessary. Moreover, the generation of models can be personalized by: specification of time limit in model generation, specification of memory limit in model generation, manual filtering of non-desired targets, establishing a limit in the number of parameters to consider in the modelling process, and/or manual filtering of non-desired algorithms or techniques. If any model exceeds any of these restriction, it is automatically discarded. The information about the discarded models comprise the inputs, the technique or algorithm, the target, and the exceeded restrictions.

Additionally, according to the performed characterization, several methods are applied to obtain models. This module has been implemented in SPSS Modeler and Python. In this way, the applied algorithms or techniques are: Anomaly detection (Chandola, Banerjee, & Kumar, 2009), apriority (Agrawal & Srikant, 1994), Bayesian network (Pearl, 2000), C5.0, Carma (Hidber, 1999), C&R Tree (Breiman, Friedman, Stone, & Olshen, 1984), Chi-squared Automatic Interaction Detector or CHAID (Kass, 1980), Cluster evaluation (based on silhouette coefficient, sum of squares error or SSE, sum of squares between or SSB, and predictor importance), COXREG (Cox, 1972), Decision List, Discriminant, Factor Analysis (PCA) (Geiger & Kubin, 2012), Generalized Linear Models, Generalized linear mixed models (Madsen & Thyregod, 2010), K-Means (MacQueen, 1967), Kohonen (Kohonen, 1982), Logistic Regression (Freedman, 2005), KNN (Pan, McInnes, & Jack, 1996), Linear modelling (Belsley, Kuh, & Welsch, 2013), neural network (Haykin, 1994), optimal binning (Usama M. Fayyad, 1993), "Quick, Unbiased, Efficient Statistical Tree" or QUEST (Loh & Shih, 1997), linear regression, Sequence, Self-learning response model or SLRMs, support vector machine (SVM), temporal casual modelling algorithms (Arnold, Liu, & Abe, 2007), time series (Box, Jenkins, & Reinsel, 2008), and Two Step cluster (Chiu, Fang, Chen, Wang, & Jeris, 2001).

The selection of the best technique is based on two criteria: the error rate of each generated method, and the correlation between the model and the target.

EXPERIMENTAL RESULTS

The proposed system was applied to several data sources related to power distribution. The data sources were related to (some columns were omitted because of a confidentiality agreement):

- Source A: Consumer historical information. This data source contains information about consumers: historical consumption data and contract information. This data source has four tables: contract information, historical data, and two parametric tables.
- Source B: Recharging point usage information. This data source contains information about consumption at a recharging point. This data source has seven tables: recharging point information, contractual information, vehicle information, consumption information, and three parametric tables.
- Source C: Generation data from different source types. This data source contains information about wind and photovoltaic generation data. This data source has three tables: historical information, source information, and a parametric table.

In the three cases, the foreign keys and interrelations between the tables were not established by constraints; the authors indicate the relations in order to make a better presentation of the data source.

After the metadata mining process and the characterization stage, the results for each data source is shown in Table I, whose information is only regarding databases. This information is evaluated by the RBES. The information about columns and tables has been omitted because of a confidentiality agreement.

In Table 1, the coefficients and indicators were calculated according to the results of previous characterization processes. In this case, all the sources showed a high rate of possibilities for application of data mining techniques. They show a high rate of cohesion and low rate of replication. The best punctuation is for time analysis and forecasting. Thus, the decision support system selected the methods related to time analysis and forecasting to be applied in the data mining stage.

These data sources were in different RDBMSs: Microsoft SQL Server, MySQL, and Oracle. The integration was performed in an H Base.

Following the IEC Standards, seventeen tables were created: Power System Resources, Measurement, Terminal, Analog, Analog Value, Analog Limit Set, Accumulator, Accumulator Value, Accumulator Limit, Accumulator Limit Set, String Measurement, String Measurement Value, Discrete, Discrete Value, Value Alias Set, Value To Alias, and Measurement Value Source. There is no table about quality of measure because there was no table about quality. Additionally, the information about the different characterization process (metadata mining) was added to the database using the tables described in the Integration of Information section.

The data mining modelling was configured to forecasting methods. This configuration is selected by the system based on the nature of the parameters and the indexes calculated in the metadata mining process. However, this situation can be changed by the user adding options for outlier detection, classification, or visualizations.

Table 1. Results of characterization of data sources

Data Source	Indicators and coefficients						
	Minable	Time analysis	Classification analysis	Fore-casting	Text analysis	Cohesion	Repli-cation
A	0.82	0.60	0.53	0.70	0.05	0.87	0
B	0.93	0.72	0.70	0.50	0.10	0.70	0.30
C	0.75	0.81	0.41	0.68	0.10	0.98	0

Table 2. Results of data mining forecasting detected parameters

Data Source	Parameter	Modelling Method	Correlation	Error
A	Authorized car dealer*	Linear Regression Generalized Linear Model	0.993	0.014
A	Hotel industry*	Regression Generalized Linear Model	0.993	0.014
A	Technical advice office*	Regression Generalized Linear Model	0.992	0.017
A	General Services*	Regression Generalized Linear Model	0.996	0.007
A	Communication office*	Regression Generalized Linear Model	0.99	0.019
A	Power Generation Company office*	Regression Generalized Linear Model	0.955	0.087
A	Authorised car dealer (without garage)*	Regression Generalized Linear Model	0.971	0.058
A	Consulting office	Neural Network (multilayer perceptron)	0.961	0.046
A	Main Power Distribution office*	Regression Generalized Linear Model	0.992	0.015
A	Power distribution office	Neural Network (multilayer perceptron)	0.977	0.046
A	Temporary employment agency office*	Regression Generalized Linear Model	0.983	0.033
B	Recharging points	Not useful model		
C	20 KW Generation Plant*	Regression Generalized Linear Model	0.993	0.014
C	80 KW Generation Plant*	Linear Regression Regression Generalized Linear Model	0.99	0.019
C	100 KW Generation Plant*	Linear Regression Regression Generalized Linear Model	0.991	0.018

*: Several modelling techniques provides similar correlation and error rates. The different techniques based on regression usually provide the same model or similar.

The results of data mining modelling in each parameter are shown in Table 2. In some cases, the system selected several methods because they had the same evaluation value; nevertheless, the different methods were ordered according to the time required for the model generation process.

A regression model was created for the Recharging point, but in the test stage the generated model showed a very high error rate. The algorithm has no information about routes or drivers.

CONCLUSION

Smart Grids and the new technologies related to information management are the future of the new smart services and applications. Several services and applications of different technological levels coexist within the current utility grid. In this sense, it is necessary to establish techniques that provide the capability to integrate information from different architecture and technological levels. These technologies increase the robustness of the management systems related to the utility grid.

The metadata mining process is focused on metadata, and taking advantage of this technology it is possible to make systems that integrate the information, according to an information standard, star, or extended-star structure. Additionally, a system for automatic modelling is provided, based on previous application of a metadata mining algorithm. In this way, this technology provides an easy-to-use and adaptive platform to integrate and model information. The models could be improved by adding new information, and performing the modelling algorithm.

In this chapter, the proposed system is applied over a power distribution system, but the future research lines may include its application of this technology over other types of databases, such as document-based and key-value databases.

ACKNOWLEDGMENTS

The authors would like to thank the Smart Business Project (SBP), which provided data sources. Additionally, the authors would like to thank the IDEA Agency for providing the funds for the project.

The authors are also appreciative of the backing of the SIIAM project, which is funded by the Ministry of Economy and Competitiveness of Spain.

REFERENCES

Agrawal, R., & Srikant, R. (1994). Fast Algorithms for Mining Association Rules in Large Databases. In *Proceedings of the 20th International Conference on Very Large Data Bases* (pp. 487–499). San Francisco, CA, USA: Morgan Kaufmann Publishers Inc. Retrieved from http://dl.acm.org/citation.cfm?id=645920.672836.

Alemu, G., & Stevens, B. (2015). 8 - The principle of metadata filtering. In *An Emergent Theory of Digital Library Metadata* (pp. 89–96). Chandos Publishing. Retrieved from http://www.sciencedirect.com/ science/article/ pii/B9780081003855000080.

Arnold, A., Liu, Y., & Abe, N. (2007). Temporal Causal Modeling with Graphical Granger Methods. In *Proceedings of the 13th ACM SIGKDD International Conference on Knowledge Discovery and Data Mining* (pp. 66–75). New York, NY, USA: ACM. https://doi.org/ 10.1145/ 1281192.1281203.

Asonitis, S., Boundas, D., Bokos, G., & Poulos, M. (2009). Semi – automated tool for characterizing news video files, using metadata schemas. In M.-A. Sicilia & M. D. Lytras (Eds.), *Metadata and Semantics* (pp. 167–178). Springer US. https://doi.org/10.1007/978-0-387-77745-0_16.

Belsley, D. A., Kuh, E., & Welsch, R. E. (2013). *Regression Diagnostics: Identifying Influential Data and Sources of Collinearity*. Hoboken, N.J: Wiley-Interscience.

Box, G. E. P., Jenkins, G. M., & Reinsel, G. C. (2008). *Time Series Analysis: Forecasting and Control* (4 edition). Hoboken, N.J: Wiley.

Breiman, L., Friedman, J., Stone, C. J., & Olshen, R. A. (1984). *Classification and Regression Trees*. Taylor & Francis.

Campos, J. P., & Silva, M. J. (2000). ActiveXML: Compound Documents for Integration of Heterogeneous Data Sources. In J. Borbinha & T. Baker (Eds.), *Research and Advanced Technology for Digital Libraries* (pp. 380–384). Springer Berlin Heidelberg. Retrieved from http://0-link.springer.com.fama.us.es/chapter/10.1007/3-540-45268-0_45.

Cao, Y., Chen, Y., & Jiang, B. (2007). A Study on Self-adaptive Heterogeneous Data Integration Systems. In L. D. Xu, A. M. Tjoa, & S. S. Chaudhry (Eds.), *Research and Practical Issues of Enterprise Information Systems II* (pp. 65–74). Springer US. Retrieved from http://0-link.springer.com.fama.us.es/chapter/10.1007/978-0-387-75902-9_7.

Chandola, V., Banerjee, A., & Kumar, V. (2009). Anomaly Detection: A Survey. *ACM Comput. Surv.*, *41*(3), 15:1–15:58. https://doi.org/10.1145/1541880.1541882.

Chen, X. d, & Liu, J. Z. (2009). Research on Heterogeneous Data Integration in the Livestock Products Traceability System. In *International Conference on New Trends in Information and Service Science, 2009. NISS '09* (pp. 969–972). https://doi.org/10.1109/NISS.2009.94.

Chen, J., Li, W., Lau, A., Cao, J., & Wang, K. (2010). Automated Load Curve Data Cleansing in Power Systems. *IEEE Transactions on Smart Grid*, *1*(2), 213–221. https://doi.org/10.1109/TSG.2010.2053052.

Chiu, T., Fang, D., Chen, J., Wang, Y., & Jeris, C. (2001). A Robust and Scalable Clustering Algorithm for Mixed Type Attributes in Large Database Environment. In *Proceedings of the Seventh ACM SIGKDD International Conference on Knowledge Discovery and Data Mining* (pp. 263–268). New York, NY, USA: ACM. https://doi.org/10.1145/502512.502549.

Cox, D. R. (1972). Regression Models and Life-Tables. *Journal of the Royal Statistical Society. Series B (Methodological)*, *34*(2), 187–220.

Fan, H., & Gui, H. (2007). Study on Heterogeneous Data Integration Issues in Web Environments. In *International Conference on Wireless Communications, Networking and Mobile Computing, 2007. WiCom 2007* (pp. 3755–3758). https://doi.org/10.1109/WICOM.2007.929.

Fengguang, X., Xie, H., & Liqun, K. (2009). Research and implementation of heterogeneous data integration based on XML. In *9th International Conference on Electronic Measurement Instruments, 2009. ICEMI '09* (pp. 4-711-4–715). https://doi.org/10.1109/ICEMI.2009.5274686.

Fermoso, A. M., Berjón, R., Beato, E., Mateos, M., Sánchez, M. A., García, M. M., & Gil, M. J. (2009). A New Proposal for Heterogeneous Data Integration to XML format. Application to the Environment of Libraries. In M.-A. Sicilia & M. D. Lytras (Eds.), *Metadata and Semantics* (pp. 143–153). Springer US. https://doi.org/ 10.1007/978-0-387-77745-0_14.

Freedman, D. (2005). *Statistical Models: Theory and Practice*. Cambridge University Press.

Gao, J., & Xiao, J. (2013). Research on Heterogeneous Data Access and Integration Model Based on OGSA-DAI. In *2013 Fifth International Conference on Computational and Information Sciences (ICCIS)* (pp. 1690–1693). https://doi.org/10.1109/ICCIS.2013.441.

Geiger, B. C., & Kubin, G. (2012). Relative Information Loss in the PCA. *arXiv:1204.0429 [Cs, Math]*, 562–566. https://doi.org/10.1109/ ITW.2012.6404738.

Guerrero, J. I., Personal, E., Parejo, A., García, A., & León, C. (2016). Forecasting the Needs of Users and Systems - A New Approach to Web Service Mining. In *The Fifth International Conference on Intelligent Systems and Applications* (pp. 96–99). Barcelona, Spain: IARIA.

Guerrero, Juan I., León, C., Monedero, I., Biscarri, F., & Biscarri, J. (2014). Improving Knowledge-Based Systems with statistical techniques, text mining, and neural networks for non-technical loss detection. *Knowledge-Based Systems*, *71*, 376–388. https://doi.org/ 10.1016/j.knosys.2014.08.014.

Guerrero, Juan Ignacio, Parejo, A., Personal, E., Biscarri, F., Biscarri, J., & Leon, C. (2016). Intelligent Information System as a Tool to Reach Unaproachable Goals for Inspectors - High-Performance Data Analysis for Reduction of Non-Technical Losses on Smart Grids (pp. 83–87). Presented at the INTELLI 2016, The Fifth International Conference on Intelligent Systems and Applications. Retrieved from https://www.thinkmind.org/index.php?view=article&articleid=intelli_2016_4_10_60123.

Hailing, W., & Yujie, H. (2012). Research on heterogeneous data integration of management information system. In *2012 International Conference on Computational Problem-Solving (ICCP)* (pp. 477–480). https://doi.org/ 10.1109/ICCPS.2012.6384220.

Han, X. b, Tian, F., & Wu, F. b. (2009). Research on Heterogeneous Data Integration in the Safety Production and Management of Coal-Mining. In *2009 First International Workshop on Database Technology and Applications* (pp. 87–90). https://doi.org/10.1109/DBTA.2009.60.

Haykin, S. (1994). *Neural Networks: A Comprehensive Foundation*. MacMillan Publishing Company.

Hidber, C. (1999). Online Association Rule Mining. In *Proceedings of the 1999 ACM SIGMOD International Conference on Management of Data* (pp. 145–156). New York, NY, USA: ACM. https://doi.org/ 10.1145/304182.304195.

Hoiles, W., & Krishnamurthy, V. (2015). Nonparametric Demand Forecasting and Detection of Energy Aware Consumers. *IEEE Transactions on Smart Grid*, *6*(2), 695–704. https://doi.org/10.1109/ TSG.2014.2376291.

Kass, G. V. (1980). An Exploratory Technique for Investigating Large Quantities of Categorical Data. *Journal of the Royal Statistical Society. Series C (Applied Statistics)*, *29*(2), 119–127. https://doi.org/ 10.2307/2986296.

Kohonen, T. (1982). Self-organized formation of topologically correct feature maps. *Biological Cybernetics*, *43*(1), 59–69. https://doi.org/ 10.1007/BF00337288.

La, Q. D., Chan, Y. W. E., & Soong, B. H. (2016). Power Management of Intelligent Buildings Facilitated by Smart Grid: A Market Approach. *IEEE Transactions on Smart Grid*, *7*(3), 1389–1400. https://doi.org/1 0.1109/TSG.2015.2477852.

León, C., Biscarri, F., Monedero, I., Guerrero, J. I., Biscarri, J., & Millán, R. (2011). Integrated expert system applied to the analysis of non-technical losses in power utilities. *Expert Systems with Applications*, *38*(8), 10274–10285. https://doi.org/10.1016/j.eswa.2011.02.062.

Li, Y., Kang, Z., & Gao, H. (2007). Automatic Data Mining by Asynchronous Parallel Evolutionary Algorithms. In L. Kang, Y. Liu, & S. Zeng (Eds.), *Advances in Computation and Intelligence* (pp. 485–492). Springer Berlin Heidelberg. Retrieved from http://0-link.springer.com.fama.us.es/ chapter/10.1007/978-3-540-74581-5_53.

Lin, Y. (2009). Study and technological realization about heterogeneous data integration based on XML Schema. In *International Conference on Test and Measurement, 2009. ICTM '09* (Vol. 2, pp. 394–397). https:// doi.org/10.1109/ICTM.2009.5413020.

Liu, H., Liu, Y., Wu, Q., & Ma, S. (2013). A Heterogeneous Data Integration Model. In F. Bian, Y. Xie, X. Cui, & Y. Zeng (Eds.), *Geo-Informatics in Resource Management and Sustainable Ecosystem* (pp. 298–312). Springer Berlin Heidelberg. Retrieved from http://0-link.springer. com.fama.us.es/chapter/10.1007/978-3-642-45025-9_31

Loh, W. Y., & Shih, Y. S. (1997). SPLIT SELECTION METHODS FOR CLASSIFICATION TREES. *Statistica Sinica*, *7*(4), 815–840.

Lu, B., & Song, W. (2010). Research on heterogeneous data integration for Smart Grid. In *2010 3rd IEEE International Conference on Computer Science and Information Technology (ICCSIT)* (Vol. 3, pp. 52–56). https://doi.org/10.1109/ICCSIT.2010.5564620.

MacQueen, J. (1967). Some methods for classification and analysis of multivariate observations. Presented at the Proceedings of the Fifth Berkeley Symposium on Mathematical Statistics and Probability, Volume 1: Statistics, The Regents of the University of California. Retrieved from http://projecteuclid.org/euclid.bsmsp/1200512992.

Madsen, H., & Thyregod, P. (2010). *Introduction to General and Generalized Linear Models*. CRC Press.

Merrett, T. H. (2001). Attribute Metadata for Relational OLAP and Data Mining. In G. Ghelli & G. Grahne (Eds.), *Database Programming Languages* (pp. 97–118). Springer Berlin Heidelberg. Retrieved from http://0-link.springer.com.fama.us.es/chapter/10.1007/3-540-46093-4_6.

Métais, E. (2002). Enhancing information systems management with natural language processing techniques. *Data & Knowledge Engineering*, *41*(2–3), 247–272. https://doi.org/10.1016/S0169-023X(02)00043-5.

Monedero, I., Biscarri, F., Guerrero, J. I., Peña, M., Roldán, M., & León, C. (2015). Detection of Water Meter Under-Registration Using Statistical Algorithms. *Journal of Water Resources Planning and Management*, *142*(1), 04015036.

Monedero, Í., Biscarri, F., León, C., Biscarri, J., & Millán, R. (2006). MIDAS: Detection of Non-technical Losses in Electrical Consumption Using Neural Networks and Statistical Techniques. In *Computational Science and Its Applications - ICCSA 2006* (pp. 725–734). Springer, Berlin, Heidelberg. https://doi.org/10.1007/11751649_80.

Pan, J. S., McInnes, F. R., & Jack, M. A. (1996). Fast clustering algorithms for vector quantization. *Pattern Recognition*, *29*(3), 511–518. https://doi.org/10.1016/0031-3203(94)00091-3.

Pearl, J. (2000). *Causality: models, reasoning, and inference*. Cambridge, U.K.; New York: Cambridge University Press.

Personal, E., Guerrero, J. I., Garcia, A., Peña, M., & Leon, C. (2014). Key performance indicators: A useful tool to assess Smart Grid goals. *Energy*, *76*, 976–988. https://doi.org/10.1016/j.energy.2014.09.015.

Richardson, P., Flynn, D., & Keane, A. (2012). Local Versus Centralized Charging Strategies for Electric Vehicles in Low Voltage Distribution Systems. *IEEE Transactions on Smart Grid*, *3*(2), 1020–1028. https://doi.org/10.1109/TSG.2012.2185523.

Ruj, S., & Nayak, A. (2013). A Decentralized Security Framework for Data Aggregation and Access Control in Smart Grids. *IEEE Transactions on Smart Grid*, *4*(1), 196–205. https://doi.org/10.1109/TSG.2012.2224389.

Şah, M., & Wade, V. (2012). Automatic metadata mining from multilingual enterprise content. *Web Semantics: Science, Services and Agents on the World Wide Web*, *11*, 41–62. https://doi.org/10.1016/j.websem. 2011.11.001.

Shi, Y., Liu, X., Xu, Y., & Ji, Z. (2010). Semantic-based data integration model applied to heterogeneous medical information system. In *2010 The 2nd International Conference on Computer and Automation Engineering (ICCAE)* (Vol. 2, pp. 624–628). https://doi.org/10.1109/ICCAE. 2010.5451697.

Sousa, T., Morais, H., Vale, Z., Faria, P., & Soares, J. (2012). Intelligent Energy Resource Management Considering Vehicle-to-Grid: A Simulated Annealing Approach. *IEEE Transactions on Smart Grid*, *3*(1), 535–542. https://doi.org/10.1109/TSG.2011.2165303.

Su, J., Fan, R., & Li, X. (2010). Research and design of heterogeneous data integration middleware based on XML. In *2010 IEEE International Conference on Intelligent Computing and Intelligent Systems (ICIS)* (Vol. 2, pp. 850–854). https://doi.org/10.1109/ICICISYS. 2010. 5658689.

Tang, J., Zhang, W., & Xiao, W. (2005). An Algebra for Capability Object Interoperability of Heterogeneous Data Integration Systems. In Y. Zhang, K. Tanaka, J. X. Yu, S. Wang, & M. Li (Eds.), *Web Technologies Research and Development - APWeb 2005* (pp. 339–350). Springer Berlin Heidelberg. Retrieved from http://0-link.springer.com.fama.us.es/ chapter/10.1007/978-3-540-31849-1_34.

Tianyuan, L., Meina, S., & Xiaoqi, Z. (2010). Research of massive heterogeneous data integration based on Lucene and XQuery. In *2010 IEEE 2nd Symposium on Web Society (SWS)* (pp. 648–652). https://doi.org/10.1109/SWS.2010.5607370.

Usama M. Fayyad, K. B. I. (1993). Multi-Interval Discretization of Continuous-Valued Attributes for Classification Learning. *Proceedings of the 13th International Joint Conference on Artificial Intelligence*, 1022–1029.

Wang, L., Wang, Z., & Yang, R. (2012). Intelligent Multiagent Control System for Energy and Comfort Management in Smart and Sustainable Buildings. *IEEE Transactions on Smart Grid*, *3*(2), 605–617. https://doi.org/10.1109/TSG.2011.2178044.

Wong, R. K. (1999). Heterogeneous data integration and presentation in multimedia database management systems. In *IEEE International Conference on Multimedia Computing and Systems, 1999* (Vol. 2, pp. 666–671 vol.2). https://doi.org/10.1109/MMCS.1999.778563.

Yi, J., & Sundaresan, N. (2000). Metadata based Web mining for relevance. In *Database Engineering and Applications Symposium, 2000 International* (pp. 113–121). https://doi.org/10.1109/IDEAS.2000.880569.

Yi, J., Sundaresan, N., & Huang, A. (2000). Metadata Based Web Mining for Topic-Specific Information Gathering. In K. Bauknecht, S. K. Madria, & G. Pernul (Eds.), *Electronic Commerce and Web Technologies* (pp. 359–368). Springer Berlin Heidelberg. Retrieved from http://0-link.springer.com.fama.us.es/chapter/10.1007/3-540-44463-7_31.

Zidan, A., & El-Saadany, E. F. (2012). A Cooperative Multiagent Framework for Self-Healing Mechanisms in Distribution Systems. *IEEE Transactions on Smart Grid*, *3*(3), 1525–1539. https://doi.org/10.1109/TSG. 2012.2198247.

BIOGRAPHICAL SKETCHES

Juan Ignacio Guerrero Alonso

Affiliation: Department of Electronic Technology. University of Seville (SPAIN)

Education: PhD, Computer Science (2011) and Master Degree in Computer Science (2006) in University of Seville (Spain). Computer Engineering Degree in University of Corduba (Spain).

Business Address: Escuela Politécnica Superior. C/Virgen de Africa nº 7. 41011 Sevilla, Spain

Research and Professional Experience: Currently, he works in University of Seville as an Assistant Professor, collaborating with department of Electronic Technology in teaching tasks and with Electronic Technology and Industrial Informatics (TIC150) research team in researching tasks. He has worked in more than 30 projects in collaboration with companies. He has several publications in reputed journals and conferences. The main research areas are related to application of big data analytics, data mining, text mining, and computational intelligence to utility sector and Smart Grids.

Professional Appointments: Assistant Professor

Publications from the Last 3 Years:

In the last three years, the author has five publications in high impact factor international scientific journals, one publication in low impact factor journal, several chapters, conferences, and seminars.

Antonio García Delgado

Affiliation: Department of Electronic Technology. University of Seville (SPAIN)

Education: B.Sc. degree in electronic physics from the University of Seville, in 1982

Business Address: Escuela Politécnica Superior. C/Virgen de Africa nº 7. 41011 Sevilla, Spain

Research and Professional Experience:
Professor of Electronic Engineering in the Electronic Technology Department since 1984. His areas of research include instrumentation, digital signal processing; fault location methods in power lines and Data analytics on Smart Grid applications.

Professional Appointments: Professor

Publications from the Last 3 Years:
4 publication in International Journals.

Enrique Personal

Affiliation: Department of Electronic Technology. University of Seville (SPAIN)

Education: industrial electronic engineering degree, automatic control and industrial electronic engineering degree, and Ph.D. degree in industrial computer science.

Business Address: Escuela Politécnica Superior. C/Virgen de Africa nº 7. 41011 Sevilla, Spain

Research and Professional Experience: Fields of interest are smart grids, fault location methods, power systems, and WSNs.

Professional Appointments: Assistant Professor, University of Seville, Spain

Publications from the Last 3 Years:
4 journal papers and 2 conference papers

Antonio Parejo Matos

Affiliation: Department of Electronic Technology. University of Seville (SPAIN)

Education: Master Degree in Electronic Engineering

Business Address: Escuela Politécnica Superior. C/Virgen de Africa n° 7. 41011 Sevilla, Spain

Research and Professional Experience: My main research areas are Smart Cities, Smart Grids and Industrial Computational Inteligence Applications. I work in University of Seville from 2015 in the research group TIC-150.

Professional Appointments: Scholarship.

Publications from the Last 3 Years: 4 research publications in aforementioned areas.

Francisco Pérez García

Affiliation: Department of Electronic Technology. University of Seville (SPAIN)

Education:
B.S. Degree in Physics (Electronic), University of Seville, 1985
Ph.D in Robotics and Digital Imaging Processing, University of Seville, 1992

Business Address: ETS Ingeniería Informática, Avenida Reina Mercedes s/n, 41012, Sevilla, Spain

Research and Professional Experience:
Dr. Francisco Pérez accepted his PhD in the field of Robotics and Digital Imaging Processing from the University of Seville, in 1992. From then, his main interest areas have been related to the field of Industrial Informatics and Industrial Communications.

In last years he has served as the Dean of the Computer Science and Engineering High Technical School (1996-2006), and as Vicerector of Teaching of the University of Seville (2007-2009).

Professional Appointments: Full Professor

Carlos León de Mora

Affiliation: Universidad de Sevilla

Education: Physic Degree. Computer Science PhD

Business Address: Escuela Politécnica Superior. C/Virgen de Africa nº 7. 41011 Sevilla, Spain

Research and Professional Experience:
Received the M.S. degree in physical electronics and the Ph.D. degree in computer science from the University of Seville, in 1991 and 1995, respectively. He is a Full Professor of Electronic Engineering with the University of Seville. His areas of research are Computational Intelligence, Knowledge-based and Cognitive systems, Data mining and Machine leraning, focusing on utility systems and complex industrial. Management. Dr. León is a senior member of the IEEE. His is co-author of more than 50 papers in JCR index Journals, has participated as author in more than 90 conferences, has co-authored 14 research book papers and has been

director of 11 PhD Thesis. His has been Director of more than 50 Research projects and have 4 patents.

Professional Appointments: Full Professor, Vicerector.

Chapter 3

ARISTON:

AN INTEGRATED EXPERT FRAMEWORK FOR OCCUPATIONAL GUIDANCE

E. J. Yannakoudakis[*]

Athens University of Economics and Business,
Athens, Greece

ABSTRACT

Within a national or indeed international socio-economic environment the ideal state of employment is defined as follows: a) Each person is employed in a sector of his preference and choice, b) the sector or still better the actual profession has a high degree of match with the personality of the employee, c) each employee is doing exactly what is needed and is also required by the society, and d) the society provides all the necessary education/training for all sectors. In other words, there is absolute balance between supply and demand of goods, services and labour. This chapter presents ARISTON, which is an integrated mathematical framework with all relevant parameters that constitute a

[*] Corresponding Author address: ASOEE, 76, Patission Street, Athens 104 34, Greece. Email: eyan@aueb.gr.

fully automated, structured expert psychometric system for occupational guidance, aiming to identify and retrieve the professions which are nearest to the personality of an individual, while at the same time quantify all nearest "neighbouring" professions.

Keywords: expert systems, personality, psychometrics, occupational guidance, career counselling, professions, work environments, ranking, clustering

INTRODUCTION

Vocational counselling and occupational guidance systems generally analyse the work personality of an individual/employee with the aim to identify the corresponding occupational preferences, professions and specialisations. When we refer to "employee" we will always imply both, the employee to be (e.g., the student), as well as the professional or generally someone already in some kind of employment. The analysis and correlation of the personality with work environments and occupational areas have been the subject of research for several years now, and the results are encouraging (Kuder 1960, Holland 1989, Yannakoudakis 2013), although the whole approach appears to involve a great deal of subjective methods and *ad hoc* decisions.

In this chapter, we define all those parameters that constitute an expert system for occupational/vocational guidance and career counselling, based on specific mathematical models which offer the basis for quantifying all levels of matching and correlations amongst the entities concerned. Evidently, the expert system has knowledge of a) all professions/specializations, b) personality types (e.g., the RIASEC scales – **R**ealistic, **I**nvestigative, **A**rtistic, **S**ocial, **E**nterprising, **C**onventional (Holland 1999)), c) the educational/training institutes, and d) the requirements of the labour market. The actual phases followed by the expert system are: 1) elicitation of the preferences and the personality of the individual by means of an appropriate questionnaire, 2) analysis of the answers given by the individual on the basis of predefined factors, 3) quantification of the degree of validity of the answers given, 4) scanning of the database with the professions and quantification of the degree of match of each of these with the personality of the individual, 5) retrieving those professions that match best with the personality, 6) linking each of the professions with faculties of higher education, 7) ranking the retrieved professions, 8) linking the retrieved professions with specific departments of higher education or training institutes, 9) synthesis of the report.

As far as reliability and validity are concerned, we adopt the well-established approaches and measures, including test-retest, split halves, r (reliability correlation-coefficient), KRr (Kuder-Richardson), Err (Standard Error Measurement), ρ (Spearman), the standard measures Z, ZP, T, $Sten$ scores, etc. However, none of these measures captures the information content of the items nor the final cluster of the professions retrieved. To this end, we adopt and reinterpret a special measure using classical information theory (Shannon 1948), which is explained later.

Another problem which appears at the phase of item definition and selection – the design of the questionnaire – is that the questions are arbitrarily defined, administered and evaluated, without reference to the concepts behind them. What we mean here is that there is no connection or linkage of the concepts behind the items with a thesaurus tree (Aitchison et al. 2003) in such a way as to determine the level at which each concept appears, whether there are broad and/or narrow terms intermixed within an item, whether the answer under elicitation is broad, narrow, related or equivalent to the major concept covered by each item, etc. We believe this is a very serious omission which ultimately affects performance but most importantly does injustice to the person answering the questions since he/she has to disambiguate the concepts in his mind before a decision can be made as to the answer that truly represents his/her world of thought.

Regarding the difficulty of questions, we doubt whether the classical approach really sheds light on the problem. Specifically, measure Δ (delta), where Nc is the number of expected (correct) answers), and N is the total number of persons involved, leaves out several important factors, including duration of each test, the degree to which the persons involved are representative of the actual final population, the complexity of the concepts within the thesaurus tree, etc.

$$\Delta = \frac{Nc}{N * 100}$$

The questions and concepts behind them have to be investigated in conjunction with the factors they represent. Our main concern here is the degree to which a given set of items can distinguish amongst factors, in other words, the degree to which a set of items can determine which factors (e.g., faculties) are prevalent and which can simply be ignored. The following measure can give us information regarding this, where M_1 is the mean of the first half of scores, M_2 is the second half of scores, σ is the standard deviation of the complete set of scores, p is the normalized score of correct answers where $q = 1 - p$. The higher the value of D (in the range $0 - 1$) the greater will be the degree of differentiation amongst the factors.

$$D = \frac{M_1 - M_2}{\sigma} \cdot p \cdot q$$

In order to assess the reliability of the psychometrics battery (a combination of tests) discussed here we compare the results between repeated administrations (test-re-test), computing the well-known reliability coefficient r using the formula:

$$r = \frac{N\sum xy - \left(\sum x\right)\left(\sum y\right)}{\sqrt{N\sum x^2 - \left(\sum x\right)^2}\ \sqrt{N\sum y^2 - \left(\sum y\right)^2}}$$

where:
    N = the total number of persons involved
    x = the scores from the first administration
    y = the scores from the second administration

The value of r ranges between -1.0 and $+1.0$, where -1.0 implies a low correlation between x και y, $+1.0$ implies a high correlation between x and y, and 0 (zero) implies no correlation between x and y.

Evidently, the time gap between successive administrations plays a very important role regarding reliability. The question thus is how we determine the ideal time gap. To this end, we propose two levels of analysis: a) Intra-administration, that is, within the realm of a specific administration that takes place within a specific time, and b) Inter-administration, that is, between different administrations that take place during different periods of time. Under a) we analyse scores from two or more different, but conceptually equivalent sets of items administered during a specific time. Under b) we analyse scores from equivalent sets of items between different administrations that took place at different periods of times. To make this clear, assume that under intra-administration we adopt the same concepts which we incorporate within different items, or the same items which are presented to the individual at different times.

Finally, the reason we adopted the word "ARISTON" is that it comes from the ancient Greek word ἄριστον meaning "The best," that is, the person who strives to excel in the work environment that matches with his personality. Thus, the ARISTON expert system aims at identifying the inherent as well as the acquired attributes of an individual and the actual work environments under which he/she can excel. We sincerely believe that each and every one of us can excel in one or more sectors, provided he/she is given the chance to explore these sectors. Finally, there is evidence to suggest that man has never been a child – Man is born as an adult (Kohnstamm, Mervielde, Halverson 1995).

DYNAMIC CLUSTERING OF PROFESSIONS

The traditional approach of identifying a category of professions (e.g., a faculty) that suits the personality of an individual is to produce a score for each pre-determined (static) category, and then simply select the one with the highest score. Unfortunately, this approach omits interdisciplinary professions and specializations, while it does not consider possible overlaps between them. So, the problem we are faced with is the selection of professions independently of the faculty or faculties they belong to, using dynamic clustering and retrieval models (Yannakoudakis 1992).

Therefore, what we need is: (a) a set of well-defined professions, each coded in a consistent manner, so that they can be integrated within the expert-database, (b) a process that selects a profession and transforms its descriptive information to appropriate data which can then be given as input to a clustering algorithm, (c) the design of an algorithm which will cluster/decompose professions, forming identifiable groups with specific properties, by adopting well-defined criteria, and (d) a process that can rank the resultant groups of professions. Clearly, the most important criteria, in our case, are related to personality factors, aptitudes and abilities in the classical sense. The techniques and models which are most appropriate for occupational guidance are commonly known as "cluster analysis" and have also been used successfully in physical and social sciences, as for example the design of database structures (Yannakoudakis 2009).

In the case of an occupational/vocational/career guidance system we have a set of elements (e.g., psychometric items), which may or may not be equivalent, and a set of corresponding measurements, that is, variables. Our aim is to use these measures in order to create a set of g clusters of professions, given N unique professions, and p variables, giving rise to a matrix of $N \times p$ measures, where g is much smaller than N, symbolically $g \ll N$.

The actual matrix processed by ARISTON involves over 2000 unique professions, each defined using 142 variables (presented later), while the occupational/vocational/career guidance psychometric batteries incorporate several tests covering over 800 thesaurus terms – concepts. The reader may visualise the matrix with the professions as follows, where each attribute is measured in the *Sten* scale:

Profession	Attribute 1	...	Attribute 142
Architect	8		5
Biophysicist	5		7
Cardiologist	6		4
...	...	...	...

The main categories of mathematical analyses are: (1) Hierarchical analysis), (2) Optimisation-partitioning), (3) Density or mode-seeking), and (4) Clumping. Following extensive study and experimentation through appropriate algorithms we have come to the conclusion that the most appropriate methods are those under category (2) Optimisation-partitioning. These methods differ from the hierarchical in that they allow the repositioning of professions from one group to another. One way to measure the total number of alternative groups is given by the following formulae (Fortier & Solomon 1966, Everitt 1993):

$$P(N,g) = \frac{g^N - \sum_{i=1}^{g-1} g_{(g-i)} P(N,i)}{g!}$$

Here, $P(N,g)$ is the number of unique partitions (groups) of the given N unique professions, each containing g clusters, while $g \geq 2$, $N \geq g$. Now, for each cluster we have:

$$g_{(g-i)} = g(g-1)(g-2)\cdots(g-i+1)$$

For example, given 19 professions ($N = 8$) and 8 groups ($g = 8$) there are 1,709,751,003,480 different partitions. Note that although most methods expect g to be given by the designer we have implemented well-established measures (e.g., Z, T, $Sten$, $Total$ professions) so that the expert system can determine the cut-off point.

Evidently, there is a need for further investigation of the aforementioned problem, in order to reduce the total number of partitions to an ideal size. One way to achieve this is to reject the incoming partition if it does not improve the current. In what follows we present the algorithm we have implemented where $G=\{g(1),\ g(2),\ldots,g(k)\}$ represent the partitions of the professions.

```
repeat
    for every g(i) in G
    do for every a in g(i)
    do begin (1)
            for ( every g(j) in G ) and ( i<>j )
            do begin (2)
                    g(i) := g(i) − {a} ;
                    g(j) := g(j) + {a} ;
                    Cur := Measure ( G′ ) ;
                    if Cur > Curmax then
                    begin (3)
                            Change := true ;
                            Record ( G′ )
                    end ; (3)
                    g(i) := g(i) + {a} ;
                    g(j) := g(j) − {a} ;
            end ; (2)
            if Change then Reform ( G, G′ ) ;
        end (1)
    until ( G = G′ )
```

Note that the temporary measure of a partition represented by $G′$ is assigned to variable Cur on the basis of one of three different procedures incorporated within the function Measure($G′$), while $Cur>Curmax$ checks for any improvement that may have been made following a comparison of the current maximum (Curmax). Besides, the function Record($G′$) records the current temporary partition $G′$, Curmax and all corresponding elements, while function Reform($G,G′$) creates the partition. In other words, a profession in $g(i)$ will only be moved to another group $g(j)$ if *Cur > Curmax*.

The expert software uses the variables/measures under each profession to measure the degree of stability of a within those already in $g(i)$ at both levels intra-$g(i)$ and inter-$g(i)$. Therefore, the degree of stability (Rubin 1967) of a profession p_i within a set G depends on:

(α) M = attraction of i towards $G-\{i\}$, where $G-\{i\}$ represents the groups of the current partition in which i is not a member.

(β) M^* = Maximum attraction of i towards any other group except G.

Although the mean stability of a profession p_i – say $O(i)$ – is the difference $M-M^*$, we use the following more precise measure:

$$O[i] = \frac{M - S^o}{1 - S^o} + \frac{S^o - M^*}{S^o}$$

Here, $i=1,...,N$ (N represents the total number of professions) and S^o represents the attraction of a profession towards the empty group. We point out that the empty group (i.e., a group without professions) becomes necessary because its absence will make it difficult to measure the degree of attraction when a group involves only one profession. So, the optimal mean stability of professions – say $\bar{M}$ –, can be calculated using all professions of the database as follows:

$$\bar{M} = \frac{1}{N} \sum_{i=1}^{N} O[i]$$

Having investigated several hypotheses regarding the distribution of multistate measures, specifically, the 142 variables in our matrix, we decided to adopt the following measure, the so called information content –

say $\pi(s)$ – of a profession s, in order to evaluate a given partition (Wallace & Boulton 1968):

$$\pi[s] = -\ln\left(\frac{n[t]}{N} \right) - \sum_d \ln\left[\frac{n[x[d,s],d,t]+1}{n[d,t]+M[d]} \right]$$

The parameters here are as follows:

s A given profession.
N Total number of professions.
$n(t)$ Total number of professions under a given category
                       (e.g., faculty).
d A multistate variable.
$x(d,s)$ The value of variable d of profession s.
$n(x(d,s),d,t)$ Total number of professions in the same category that have
                       the same value for variable d.
$n(d,t)$ Total number of professions under a given category
                       with known values under variable d.
$M(d)$ Total number of states of variable d.

In our interpretation of the information content, $\pi(s)$, we claim that it represents the amount of information required for the "coding" of a given profession on the variables which are assigned values *a priori*. Thus, the overall measure for all N professions of the set G'' gives us the overall information content – say Π – which becomes necessary for the coding of all professions as follows:

$$\Pi = \sum_{s=1}^{n} \pi[s]$$

In fact, the model presented above enables us to determine the probability for a given profession s that is classed under a given category g, with a known distribution to have specific values under a given set of variables (e.g., one or more values from the set of 142 variables). Therefore, the question "How can we measure the degree of match between two professions" becomes "How can we measure the degree of consistency – match of a set of professions within a given category." Here, the algorithm we have implemented is similar to the one presented above with the difference that in this case the algorithm retrieves source values directly for the matrix (Yannakoudakis 2009).

EVALUATION OF THE RESULTING GROUPS OF PROFESSIONS

Evidently, the data we have at our disposal are specific and include: a) groups of professions, b) groups of items under well-defined factors, c) groups of answers that are given by an individual, and d) measures already collected from previous cases of individuals, classified by age, sex, geographic area, multistate variables, etc. The latter are otherwise known as norms. The ultimate objective is to retrieve professions which are compatible with the personality of the person under examination (Kuder 1960, Holland 1999, Yannakoudakis 1999, 2013). Therefore, the frequencies of occurrence of the elements/data involved as well as their distributions make it necessary to adopt specific mathematics for matrix manipulation, clustering, hierarchical, and ranking techniques. In order to estimate the distribution r we adopt the following formula:

$$\operatorname{var} \hat{R} = V(r) = \frac{1-f}{n\overline{X}^2} \cdot \frac{\sum\limits_{i=1}^{n}(y_i - rx_i)^2}{n-1}$$

Note that when the mean population value $\overline{X}$ is unknown it can be estimated using the mean value $\overline{x}$ of the sample. If we assume that p_n is the frequency of occurrence of an element with rank n and C_n is the cost of using the element, then the mean cost of this element will be:

$$\overline{M}_{C_n} = \sum p_n C_n$$

Here, the concept "cost" is related to the rank of an element (e.g., a profession), implying that the lower its rank the cheaper the element will be and therefore closer to the personality of the individual. Clearly, the problem is related to the ranking of that subset of the professions retrieved from the database where rank 1 is the best and rank $n<<N$ is the worst. Mandelbrot suggests methods for minimising the cost using variations of the p_n distribution (Mandelbrot, 1952, 1953).

Another very important topic related to ranking is the so called Zipfian distribution (Zipf 1949) which can predict the frequency of the elements with rank k using the following formula, given a population of N elements, and s as the value of the exponent characterizing the distribution:

$$f(N,s,k) = \frac{1/k^s}{\sum_{n=1}^{N}(1/n^s)}$$

In simple terms, Zipf's law states that the frequencies of certain events are inversely proportional to their rank r, while this frequency is given approximately by f(r) $\cong$ 0.1/r. Mandelbrot came along to generalize Zipf's law, also known as the Pareto-Zipf law (Debowski Lukasz 2000), which proposes modelling by distributions of hyperbolic type and is linked to the classical entropy – information theory, leading to a property of stability and exibility (Harremoes & Topsoe 2002). In the same spirit, Shannon proposed the measure of entropy (Shannon, 1948) and therefore the redundancy of a discrete set, in our case a set of professions $i=1,\ldots,n$, each having a probability of occurrence p_i, using the following well-known formula where k is a constant:

$$H = -k \sum_{i=1}^{n} p_i \cdot \log_2(p_i)$$

Let us assume that t denotes the total number of unique elements, ranked in ascending cost order 1,...,t, and n_r denotes the frequency of occurrence of an element within a set of n elements. If the absolute frequency of occurrence of element r is n_r and the relative frequency f_r is n_r/n, then:

$$n = \sum_{r=1}^{t} n_r$$

Besides, we can compute a very important constant – say c –, where:

$$c = f_r r^{\alpha}$$

Constant α is related to the steepness of the log-log graph and tends towards the unit. When α is 1, the following holds, where c can be interpreted as the relevant frequency of an element with rank 1:

$$n_r = \frac{cn}{r}$$

THE PARAMETERS OF THE GUIDANCE SYSTEM

Evidently, human behaviour is determined by inherent as well as acquired personality traits and factors which can be measured with a high degree of certainty. To this end, it becomes necessary to define precisely all psychometric scales/factors and tests that constitute an integrated system for occupational/vocational/career guidance.

The psychometric tests we have implemented in the form of batteries and tested thoroughly by administering these to over 100,000 individuals incorporate the following 9 different tests: a) Truth scales, b) Personality traits (www.aristontest.eu), c) Aptitudes – Abilities (Mathematical, Linguistic, Mechanical, Diagrammatic), d) Self-esteem (Coopersmith 1959), e) Locus of Control (Rotter 1975, Gerrig & Zimbardo 2012), f) Work Personality (Holland 1999), g) Preferences, h) Motivation, i) Academic Faculties (www.aristontest.eu). The actual parameters and scales are presented in Table 1.

Table 1. Parameters and Scales

1.	Age group	2.	Country group
3.	Sex	4.	Duration of RIASEC scales
5.	Duration of Self-esteem scales	6.	Duration of Locus of control scales
7.	Duration of Faculty scales	8.	Truth score – Overall
9.	Truth score – RIASEC scales	10.	Truth score – Self-esteem scales
11.	Truth score – Locus of control scales	12.	Truth score - Motive scales
13.	Truth score – Faculty scales	14.	Probability of errors in the answers
15.	Mathematical aptitudes	16.	Linguistic aptitudes
17.	Mechanical aptitudes	18.	Diagrammatic reasoning
19.	Recognition of work	20.	Autonomy at work
21.	Prospects for promotion	22.	Exercise of influence & authority
23.	Security, stability & comfort	24.	Financial rewards
25.	RIASEC – Realistic	26.	RIASEC – Investigative
27.	RIASEC – Artistic	28.	RIASEC – Social
29.	RIASEC – Enterprising	30.	RIASEC – Conventional
31.	Internal locus of control	32.	External locus of control
33.	General self-esteem	34.	Esteem by others
35.	Esteem by the parents/close relatives	36.	Esteem at school/academic environment
37.	Educational Sciences	38.	Security Services
39.	Services & Tourism	40.	Computing Sciences
41.	Architecture & Town Planning	42.	Economics, Business &Administration

43. Technology & Engineering	44. Sport Sciences
45. Natural Sciences	46. Agricultural Sciences
47. Health Sciences	48. Life Sciences
49. Earth & Environmental Sciences	50. Communication & Documentation
51. Mathematics & Statistics	52. Law
53. Arts	54. Social Sciences
55. Humanities	56. Variability of factors
57. Consistency of factors	58. Differentiation of factors
59. Energetic	60. Domineering
61. Arresting	62. Self-confident
63. Ambitious	64. Optimistic
65. Acquisitive	66. Sociable
67. Adventurous	68. Resourceful
69. Excitement-seeking	70. Enthusiastic
71. Forceful	72. Assertive
73. Efficient	74. Methodical
75. Obedient	76. Conforming
77. Conservative	78. Orderly
79. Thrifty	80. Conscientious
81. Thorough	82. Careful
83. Down-to-Earth	84. Inhibited
85. Adamant	86. Uncompromising
87. Agreeable	88. Persuasive
89. Co-operative	90. Reliable
91. Tactful	92. Warm
93. Kind	94. Understanding
95. Helpful	96. Friendly
97. Generous	98. Patient
99. Ideologue	100. Empathic
101. Critical	102. Precise
103. Cautious	104. Retiring
105. Introspective	106. Intellectual
107. Curious	108. Analytical
109. Rational	110. Sceptic
111. Self-governing	112. Radical
113. Complex	114. Unassuming
115. Impulsive	116. Intuitive

Table 1. (Continued)

117. Visionary	118. Expressive
119. Open	120. Sensitive
121. Emotional	122. Independent
123. Complicated	124. Original
125. Nonconforming	126. Disorderly
127. Imaginative	128. Dreamer
129. Robust	130. Materialistic
131. Reserved	132. Reasonable
133. Adaptable	134. Self-effacing
135. Natural	136. Insightful
137. Persistent	138. Hard-headed
139. Inflexible	140. Self-opinionated
141. Genuine	142. Realistic

In order to measure the degree on sincerity in the answers given by an individual we calculate specific truth scores by analysing the following data collected by the expert system, classifying these by age, sex, and geographic area (e.g., country):

a) Time spent per question
b) Anticipated time per concept
c) Time per factor
d) Time per test
e) Time per battery
f) Predictability of an answer
g) Predictability of a factor/trait
h) Predictability of a sequence of answers
i) Predictability of contradicting concepts
j) Predictability of established attitudes to life

Another very important factor in psychometrics is related to the duration of the administration of the batteries. To this end, we keep track of the time per test, as well as per item, storing these for further processing.

By analysing the duration we can come to certain very important conclusions not only about the *biorhythm* of the individuals tested, but also about the degree of difficulty of the concepts behind the items of the batteries.

In what follows we present sample questions, exactly as they appear on the screen of the computer, so that the user can appreciate the form and method of appearance of the items.

```
Do you need encouragement, in order to become more active

1. Often
2. Sometimes
3. Seldom
4. Almost never
```

```
Which letter of the alphabet completes the sequence at *
C   F   I   *   O

1. J
2. K
3. L
4. M
```

```
Which number does the * represent in the following series

3   7   10   17   27   *
```

```
If the right hand is near the arrow, then which foot is near the ball

1. Left
2. Right
```

```
Would you like to watch a TV program on how light makes us see
```

A REALISTIC EXAMPLE

In order to demonstrate the model discussed here we present indicative sections from a real report created by the expert system for a person aged 17 years old, who is expected to enter a University Department for an undergraduate course. All the sections presented below are actual copies from the report which is created by the expert system without any human intervention. Note that the model discussed in this paper can be equally applied for personnel assessment and selection, including University staff and students (Yannakoudakis 2013).

Figure 1 shows the distribution of the RIASEC scales (work environments), where the dominant type is the Enterprising, implying, amongst other, that the person is in a position to persuade people.

Figure 2 shows the Self-esteem scales where the Environment type appears to be on the low side.

Figure 3 shows the Locus of control scales with a balanced distribution, implying that the person is in a position to control the work environment, since the dominant scale is the internal locus of control.

Figure 4 shows the motive scales related to the work environments.

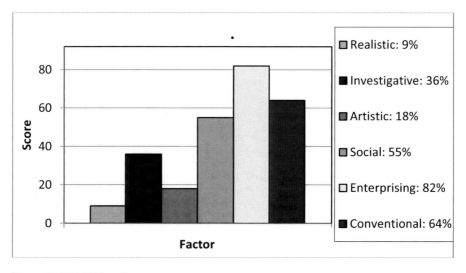

Figure 1. RIASEC scales.

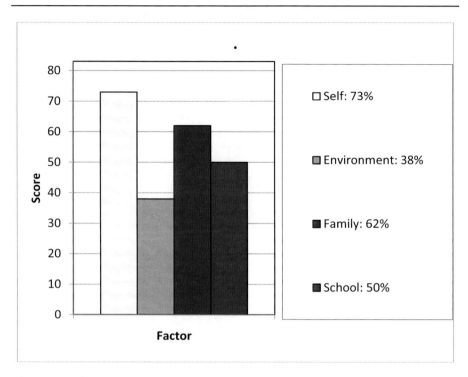

Figure 2. Self-esteem scales.

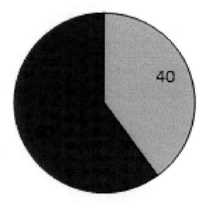 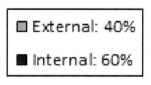

Figure 3: Locus of control scales

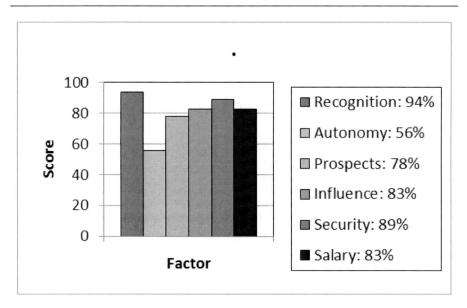

Figure 4. Motive scales.

Figure 5 shows the aptitude scales where the Linguistic type appears dominant.

Figure 6 shows the distribution of the scores under the 19 faculty scales where the dominant scales are: Education, Security, Services, Computing, Architecture, and Economics.

Figure 7 presents the ranking of the occupational – personality factors (the actual inclinations) using standardised scores according to the theory of Zipf-Mandelbrot discussed earlier. Here, the personalised distribution is shown by the Zipf curve (a non-equiprobable distribution), while the theoretical distribution, which can be considered as the minimum distribution, is shown by the Mandelbrot curve.

Table 2 shows the enterprising (dominant) scales in descending *Sten* score order.

Table 3 shows the scores of selected psychometric scales, each analysed and compared with the corresponding norm scores with an appropriate description using the following coding: **VH** (Very High), **H** (High), **N** (Normal), **L** (Low), **VL** (Very Low).

Table 4 shows the ranks and the corresponding faculties which are related to the personality of the individual.

Table 5 shows the ranks and the corresponding groupings (total of 9) created by the algorithm discussed earlier where the group {Security, Services} appears with the maximum cardinality, indicating in effect the dominance of this group.

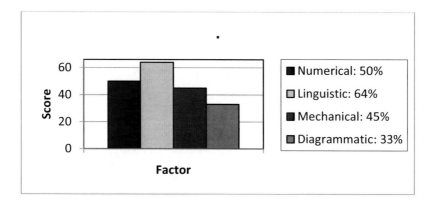

Figure 5. Aptitude scales.

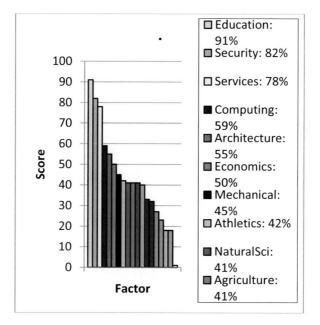

Figure 6. Faculty scales.

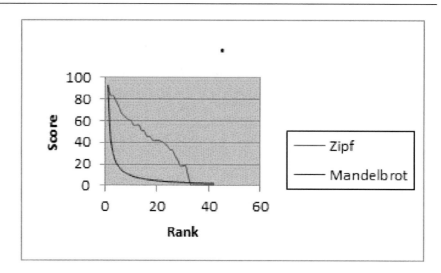

Figure 7. Ranking of occupational – personality factors.

Table 2. Enterprising scales

O/N	Factor	Score
1	Energetic	7
2	Domineering	7
3	Arresting	7
4	Self-confident	7
5	Ambitious	7
6	Optimistic	7
7	Acquisitive	7
8	Sociable	6
9	Adventurous	4
10	Resourceful	4
11	Excitement-seeking	3
12	Enthusiastic	3
13	Forceful	3
14	Assertive	3

Table 3. Selected psychometric scales (Norm scores)

O/N	Factor	Score	Norm
1	Enterprising type	82	H
2	Conventional type	64	VH
3	Social type	55	N
4	Investigative type	36	L
5	Artistic type	18	VL
6	Realistic type	9	VL
7	Self-Esteem & awareness	73	N
8	Esteem by family - close relatives	62	N
9	Esteem at school - academic environment	50	N
10	Esteem by environment	38	VL
11	External locus of control	40	L
12	Internal locus of control	60	VH
13	Educational Sciences	91	VH
O/N	Factor	Score	Norm
14	Security Services	82	VH
15	Services & Tourism	78	VH
16	Computing Sciences	59	N
17	Architecture & Town Planning	55	H
18	Economics, Business & Administration	50	H
19	Technology & Engineering	45	N
20	Sport Sciences	42	N
21	Natural Sciences	41	N
22	Agricultural Sciences	41	N
23	Health Sciences	41	N
24	Life Sciences	40	N
25	Earth & Environmental Sciences	33	L
26	Communication & Documentation	32	N
27	Mathematics & Statistics	27	L
28	Law	23	L
29	Arts	18	L
30	Social Sciences	18	VL
31	Human Sciences	1	VL

Table 4. Faculties and Ranks

Rank	Faculty
1	Services
2	Security
3	Education
3	Education
4	Education
5	Security
5	Security
5	Services
5	Services
5	Services
5	Services
6	Security
6	Security
6	Security
6	Security
6	Services
6	Services
7	Computing
7	Computing
7	Architecture
8	Computing
8	Computing
9	Architecture
9	Architecture

Table 5. Grouping by rank

Rank	Group	Cardinality
1	{ Services }	1
2	{ Security }	1
3	{ Education }	2
4	{ Education }	1
5	{ Security, Services }	6
6	{ Security, Services }	6
7	{ Computing, Architecture }	3
8	{ Computing }	2
9	{ Architecture }	2

Table 6. Final list of faculties and professions

Rank	Faculty	Profession
1	Services	Event organiser – Manager
2	Security	Security officer
3	Education	Educator – teacher
3	Education	Pre-school education specialist
4	Education	Teacher
5	Security	Military training officer
5	Security	Police officer
5	Services	Home economics & bionomics
5	Services	Hotel management
Rank	**Faculty**	**Profession**
5	Services	Tourism development specialist
5	Services	Tourist business manager
6	Security	Army officer
6	Security	Aviation officer
6	Security	Military recruiting officer
6	Security	Naval officer
6	Services	Historian – Guide
6	Services	Public relations - tourist business
7	Computing	Computer scientist - industry
7	Computing	Information systems designer
7	Architecture	Interior decorator
8	Computing)	Cognitive sciences specialist
8	Computing	Computer scientist - electronic systems
9	Architecture	Architect – decorator
9	Architecture	Digital signal processing specialist (ID)

Table 6 shows the final list of the faculties and the corresponding professions related to the personality of the individual. Here we see that the expert system has retrieved a total of 24 professions (ID denotes an interdisciplinary profession), under 5 faculties (Services, Security, Education, Computing, and Architecture). Note that the system has excluded the Economics faculty because of its distance from the nearest neighbourhood groups. However, the software designed enables the administrator to define several parameters (minimum and maximum) on the basis of the *Rank, Z, ZP, T, Sten*, the total number of professions to be retrieved, etc. Therefore, the counsellor can advise the candidate to investigate further the profession from the 1st rank (Event organiser – Manager), or indeed any of the professions from the 2nd rank onwards, given that they all match with the personality of the candidate.

RELIABILITY – VALIDITY

Having accumulated over 100,000 representative real cases of individuals aged 14 – 65 years old we decided to run reliability – validity tests and compare with the previous set of cases used for the normalization of ARISTON (Papadourakis 2013). The results presented in Table 7 show a high correlation between the faculty scales and the corresponding Kuder scales (Yannakoudakis 1999), particularly amongst the faculties: Arts, Law, Social Sciences, Communication & Documentation, Life Sciences, Natural Sciences, Earth & Environmental Sciences, Mathematics & Statistics, Computing Sciences, Architecture & Town Planning, Agricultural Sciences, and Health Sciences.

Table 8 shows the correlation coefficients between the RIASEC scales and the corresponding Kuder scales.

In conclusion, the model presented here has proved to be highly reliable, and all coefficients related to the identification of faculties/professions that match with the personality of an individual are significantly higher than the minimum requirement of 0.7. Besides, we have evidence to suggest that when an individual attends a course of study that is in congruence with his/her personality, then the rate of learning becomes much greater, particularly when the teacher/educator imparts knowledge according to the learning profile of the individual (Yannakoudakis et al. 2014).

Finally, it is clear that the implementation of the occupational/ vocational/career guidance model discussed here requires knowledge of statistics, mathematics, psychometrics, but above all computer programming skills as well as knowledge of expert database systems. More specifically, for the implementation of the algorithms it is necessary to adopt a programming language with built-in mathematical functions and, ideally, matrix manipulation functions. For the user interface it becomes necessary to adopt a language that enables the design of user-friendly interfaces for the presentation of the questions and the collection of the answers. Regarding the creation of the report, we have designed a specialized tagging system that automates the synthesis of a .pdf file which is sent to the counsellor for presentation to the person under investigation.

Table 7. Faculty scales – Validity measurements

Faculty scales	Kuder scales	Coefficients
Humanities	Literary	.75
Arts	Artistic	.89
Law	Persuasive	.88
Social Sciences	Social services	.90
Communication & Documentation	Literary	.82
Economics, Business & Administration	Persuasive	.79
Life Sciences	Scientific	.81
Natural Sciences	Scientific	.83
Earth & Environmental Sciences	Outdoor	.88
Mathematics & Statistics	Computational	.84
Computing Sciences	Computational	.90
Educational Sciences	Persuasive	.72
Technology & Engineering	Mechanical	.79
Architecture & Town Planning	Artistic	.80
Agricultural Sciences	Outdoor	.88
Health Sciences	Social services	.83
Sport Sciences	Outdoor	.78
Services and Tourism	Clerical	.71
Security Services	Social services	.70

Table 8. RIASEC scales – Validity measurements

RIASEC scales	Kuder scales	Coefficients
Realistic	Mechanical	.81
Investigative	Scientific	.87
Artistic	Artistic	.90
Social	Social services	.89
Enterprising	Persuasive	.85
Conventional	Clerical	.82

REFERENCES

Aitchison, J., Bawden, D., Gilchrist, A., (2003). Thesaurus Construction and Use: A Practical Manual. *Routledge.*

Coopersmith, S., (1959). A method for determining types of self-esteem. *The Journal of Abnormal and Social Psychology*, Vol 59(1), 87-94.

Debowski, Lukasz, (2000). Zipf's Law: What and Why?. *Institute of Computer Science*, Polish Academy of Sciences.

Everitt, B. S., (1993). Cluster analysis. *Heinemann.*

Fortier, J. J., Solomon, H., (1966). Clustering procedures, *Proc. Symposium on Multivariate Analysis, Dayton Ohio (P. R. Krishnaian, ed.), Academic Press*, 493-506.

Gerrig, R., Zimbardo, P. G., (2012). Psychology and life (20th ed.). *Boston, MA: Allyn & Bacon.*

Harremoes, P., Topsoe, Flemming, (2002). Zipf's law, hyperbolic distributions and entropy loss. *ISIT*, Switzerland, June 30 - July 5.

Holland, J. L., (1989). Making vocational choices: A theory of careers. *Prentice-Hall.*

Holland, J. L., (1999). Making career choices: A theory of personality types and work environments. *Englewood Cliffs, Prentice-Hall.*

Kohnstamm, G. A., Mervielde, I., Besevegis, E., Halverson, C. F., (1995). Tracing the Big Five in parents' free descriptions of their children. *European Journal of Personality*, 9, 283-304.

Kuder, G. F., (1960). The preference record - Vocational form C. *SRA, Chicago.*

Mandelbrot, B., (1952). An information theory of the structure of language based upon the theory of the statistical matching of messages and coding. *Proc. of the London Symposium.* Also, In: Jackson Willis (Ed.), *Proc. of a Symposium on applications of communication theory*, London, Butterworth, 1953.

Papadourakis, G. M., Foudoulaki, E., Yannakoudakis, J. E., Alogdianaki, M., (2013). An Expert Systems Approach to Career Counselling. *8th International Conference "New Horizons in Industry, Business and Education"*, 71-76, Perle Hotel, Chania, Greece, 29-30 August 2013.

Rotter, J. B., (1975). Some problems and misconceptions related to the construct of internal versus external control of reinforcement. *Journal of Consulting and Clinical Psychology*, 43: 56–67.

Rubin, J., (1967). Optimal classification into groups: an approach for solving the taxonomy problem. *Journal of Theoretical Biology*, Vol. 15, 103-144.

Shannon, C. E., (1948). A mathematical theory of communication. *Bell Systems Technical Journal*, Vol. 27, 379-423, July 1948, and 623-656, October 1948.

Wallace, C. S., Boulton, D. M., (1968). An information measure for classification. *Computer Journal*, Vol. 11, 185-194.

Yannakoudakis, E. J., Flokas, E., (1992). Attribute decomposition as an aid to database design. *Proc. HERMES Conference on Mathematics & Informatics*, 113-136, 25-26.

Yannakoudakis, E. J., (1999). Vocational preferences of young people: The future of a nation. *Scientific American* (in Greek), Volume A, Issue 5, 88-91.

Yannakoudakis, E. J., (2009). Design and management of database systems (in Greek). *Mpenou Publishers*, 2nd Edition, Chapter 6.

Yannakoudakis, E. J., (2013). A Psychometrics-based Approach for the Assessment of University Staff and Students. *Journal of the World Universities Forum*, Volume 6, Issue 1, 33-42.

Yannakoudakis, J. E., Yannakoudakis, H. E., Yannakoudakis, I. E., Papadourakis, G. M., (2014). Using an Expert System to Automatically Map the Learning Profile of Individuals. *The Sixth International Conference on Mobile, Hybrid, and On-line Learning, eLmL*, 8-13, March 23 - 27, Barcelona, Spain, 2014.

Zipf, G. K., (1949). Human behavior and the principle of least effort. *Addison-Wesley*, Reading, MA.

ABOUT THE AUTHOR

Emmanuel J. Yannakoudakis BSc, PhD, CEng, CITP, FBCS

ΟΙΚΟΝΟΜΙΚΟ   ATHENS UNIVERSITY
ΠΑΝΕΠΙΣΤΗΜΙΟ   OF ECONOMICS
ΑΘΗΝΩΝ   AND BUSINESS

Πατησίων 76, 104 34 Αθήνα. Τηλ.: 210 8203 355, 210 8203 356
76, Patission Street, Athens 104 34 Greece
Tel.: (+30) 210 8203 355, 210 8203 356

Professor of Computer Science, Consultant/Adviser of the European Union since 1982, Associate Editor/Referee for several international journals, External examiner for Ph.D. candidates throughout Europe and Africa. The subjects taught include Computer Science, Databases, Programming Languages, Expert Systems, and Psychometric Information Systems. Studied Computer Science and obtained his PhD in Computer Science in 1979 from the University of Bradford, England, where he taught at both Undergraduate and Postgraduate Schools (1975-1989). He is Fellow of the British Computer Society (FBCS), Chartered Engineer (C.Eng.), and Chartered Information Technology Professional (CITP).

Has directed several major research projects and has designed several information systems and databases in the areas of Databases, Psychometric tests, Vocational counselling, Information retrieval, Library automation, etc. He was one of the first programmers to implement psychometric testing back in 1974. Has designed special information systems for three Presidents of the Hellenic Republic. Has published 55 papers at International Journals, 74 papers at Conference Proceedings, and 19 Books some of which are with International publishers.

---

* http://www.aueb.gr/Users/yannakoudakis/english/
E-mail: eyan@aueb.gr

INDEX